SALES TALKS

SALES TALKS

Six Secrets to Winning Presentations, Effective Closes, and Think-on-Your-Feet Tactics That Seal Deals

GREG UPAH

To my Dad

ISBN 13: 978-1-59298-810-5
Library of Congress Catalog Number: 2017919268
Printed in the United States of America
First Printing: 2018
22 21 20 19 18   5 4 3 2 1

Cover and interior design by Ryan Scheife, Mayfly Design
Edited by Marly Cornell

BEAVER'S POND
PRESS

Beaver's Pond Press, Inc.
7108 Ohms Lane
Edina, MN 55439–2129
(952) 829-8818
www.BeaversPondPress.com

To order, visit www.ItascaBooks.com
or call (800) 901-3480. Reseller discounts available.

Visit gregupah.com.

CONTENTS

NOTE FROM THE AUTHOR

This kind of book is usually written by someone in the midst of a thriving career. I certainly didn't expect to contract multiple sclerosis but, at age forty-three, I did. For six years I worked through mobility, balance, and fatigue issues to become the senior institutional sales executive at Merrill Lynch Asset Management, then one of the largest asset managers in the world and now part of BlackRock. The travel demands, stress, and pressure that I once thrived on made it unwise and difficult to continue in my position, so I went on long-term disability. I'm now an associate at Bank of America, which acquired Merrill Lynch, and I've been treated exceedingly well.

Sales Talks is not about overcoming adversity, though it could be. My new role has given me time to reflect on what helped me and my sales team achieve great success. Here, I share techniques that hold enduring relevance to the challenges and opportunities of today's business environment. This book is designed to give any salesperson ideas to improve the product-customer fit, enhance persuasion, and make the sale. I hope it does so for you.

Greg Upah

PREFACE

Jump Off the Capabilities Bandwagon

I n business, effectively persuasive face-to-face communications can produce sales success as well as career success. The focus of this book is on how to achieve both of those outcomes.

People buy what someone else is selling mostly because it best suits their particular "matter at hand." That is the essence of customer relevance, and it is at the core of effective persuasion. However, chances are that if you look at any written sales presentation, there is more said about the presenter's company and credentials than about how those attributes solve the customer's matter at hand. Recent surveys and plenty of anecdotal evidence suggest that, though customer relevance is highly valued, it is a quality that buyers often find missing in sales presentations.

If I were doing a seminar on persuasive presentations for your organization, the first question I would ask is how much of your written presentation material talks about what your company does rather than demonstrating how your company can help the customer. Your customer wants to know how what you offer solves their problem. "Don't boast about your company: rather tell us the problem you're solving," is the advice of Chris Anderson, head of TED.[1]

Presenters need to spend more time perfecting their understanding of their customer than perfecting their pitch. Yes, there are things your company does that are commendable and distinctive. But it is not the good things you do that count most; it is the ones that are most meaningful to the customer. A major reason presentations fail is that they are based on superficial, boilerplate, or just plain wrong information. What presenters assume they know often turns out to be incorrect. So jump off the capabilities bandwagon long enough to understand the heart of your customer's matter at hand, and constructively center your presentation on how you will go about satisfying that matter.

This process is about being insight-driven not just information/data-driven. Customer insights are out there to be discovered. They include what is notable, stand out, or mission-critical to your company's customers. Beneath-the-surface issues that are decision-significant to the customer are not typically found in demographic or customer relationship management profiles, big data, or even in requests for proposals. They may not even be found in your initial due-diligence efforts. The decision-significant issues are found by asking your customers the right kinds of open-ended questions, then following up and listening. And this quest for insights continues up to and through the beginning of the face-to-face presentation. With that foundation, presenters can cut to the chase, which is what customers want anyway. Create proposals to clients that are surgical, not shotgun. Address needs in a precise, nongeneric way, putting a sharp, insightfully informed focus on what is meaningful to the client. Tailor every action to achieve the perfect product-customer fit, because the seller who creates the best fit wins.

A foundation in customer insights informs everything in a presentation from its customer relevance to the presenter's confidence, and to the ability to constructively make the necessary alterations in response to client feedback that will enhance the match between what sellers offer and what buyers need.

Great preparation provides the initial level of client relevance to have a chance to succeed. How presenters respond to what happens in the meeting room and deal with objections and changing circumstances is, all else being equal, what determines whether or not they will ultimately succeed.

This book provides classic and current stories about actual presentations that suggest techniques for finding insights, being relevantly connected to the customer, and confidently and constructively overcoming obstacles—even the proposal-killing ones. Soft skills play a huge role. The lack of soft skills, such as listening, self-confidence, and adaptability, remains among the major reasons salespeople fail. A story-based perspective is provided here because one of the best ways to improve those skills is by learning what has worked for others.

INTRODUCTION

The Seller Who Best Suits the Client Wins

L et me tell you a story about making a long-distance sales call on a unique client.

The client was a multibillionaire, the principal shareholder of a major Australian conglomerate and one of the wealthiest people in the world. Incidentally, he was well known as an extravagant gambler. Whether he won or lost millions at the casino, he left enormous tips for the staff on his way out.

After traveling ten thousand miles in thirty hours, capped by a sixty-minute helicopter ride to his ninety-thousand-acre ranch north of Sydney (one of his several ranches that together covered an area equivalent to 40 percent of England), I was now sitting in his home, awaiting my much-anticipated, first-time meeting with this man.

This ranch was no outpost in the outback. It was dominated by a polo field worthy of the best players in the world. Two of those elite players were playing in a match when we arrived. One of the other players on the field was the billionaire himself.

When the game ended, he came directly to the ranch house, and sat down at the opposite end of a sofa from me. After all of the briefings from his chief lieutenants, it was time to present our firm's proposal for managing a very large pool of his assets.

I handed him the presentation book I had prepared. He glanced at it and discarded it.

I stopped referring to the document and immediately got to the point about how we proposed to invest his money. He asked no questions.

Barely three minutes later, he made this statement: "This is not what I'm looking for." He then stood and began to walk out of the room.

This story could have been a postmortem of what not to do in an investment sales presentation and ended right there as our prospective client walked out the door. But it didn't end there. We won that account and I'll tell you how we did it.

There is much more to say about the reasons for his startling and swift rejection of the proposal, the rest of the saga, and the tipping point that occurred in the waning seconds of his departure that enabled the situation to turn from failure to success. I will talk about all of that, but before I do let me point out that, from beginning to end, this particular story illustrates almost every facet of what it takes to be persuasive and successful in face-to-face presentations in financial services, and in many other industries as well.

What it takes can be summarized simply: The reasons audiences buy what presenters sell is mostly because they believe it will help them deal with their matter at hand in ways most beneficial to them. The more an investment presentation is tailored to what is meaningful to the client, the more persuasive it will be. The priority for every presenter is to be exacting and insightful about the key dimensions of the client's objectives. That understanding should drive an organic, ground-up process in which the presenter continuously and confidently alters their proposal in response to new information, until the desired fit is achieved. The perfect fit is the goal, and the seller that best achieves that fit wins.

Six secrets to achieve the fit that wins

When making a sales presentation, information alone is never enough. To be optimally persuasive, you need insights about your customer's objectives and motivations, and soft skills and techniques that produce the "think on your feet" responsiveness needed to confidently overcome obstacles and adapt to changing circumstances. To that end, six not-so-secret directives are integrated into classic and current stories in this book with a perspective that is further reinforced in each example. The advice offered is less about "the what" or "the why," and much more about "the how." Following the principles described either separately or in combination will help any presenter be more persuasive.

1) Be relevant first.

Think about the goal of the sales process as achieving the perfect fit between every aspect of your proposal and your client's most critical objectives. Don't jump on the capabilities bandwagon by listing your capabilities in isolation. Instead call out your *relevant capabilities*, drawing clear and consistent lines to your client's goals and objectives.

Audit your written presentation for client relevance. If you are 80 percent seller-focused, reengage your customers and shift the balance back to them. Vary your presentation from one prospect to the next because different customers buy the exact same product for different reasons. Design and use your own one-page evidence matrix (or a similar device) as a focal point to efficiently make your case.

2) Be insightful, not just informed.

There is always something below the surface of customer motivations that determines the success of all downstream marketing efforts. Those client insights are found in interviews, not in big data, CRM profiles, or RFPs (requests for proposals). Uncover those insights by asking the right open-ended questions. *Listen* closely, notice what is commonly mentioned, and follow up for more valuable answers. You will be more believable and liked and thought of as more capable when you ask and listen.

3) Lay out your logic, verify, and don't assume.

Lay out the logic of your presentation upfront. Ask the client to *verify* your understanding of their objectives *and* expectations, and confirm that your approach is on the right track. *Never assume* that you have it right.

4) Foster, inspire, and earn confidence.

Develop and foster your personal level of conviction and belief in what you offer clients. Base your confidence on the attributes of your product and the strength of its *fit* with what has meaning to your client.

Inspiring confidence means assuring clients that you will fulfill the expectations you create. There is no better confidence-builder than knowing that you are surgically addressing the correct problem (and no worse feeling than learning that you wasted your time and resources focusing on the wrong one). Earn your client's confidence by doing what you say you will do.

5) Adapt and alter constructively.

Make alterations as necessary to meet your client's objectives, even as circumstances change. Successfully adapting to customer objections requires the proper demeanor and soft skills such as acknowledging your client's concerns, showing with facts how and why you can address those concerns, being diplomatic not defensive, and constructive not confrontational.

6) Extend the fit to other constituents.

Consider conducting your own research to help your client better understand their own customers, employees, internal management, family members, and other constituents. Tailor your proposal and adapt as needed to fit more than one audience. Take an advisory posture. Customers appreciate insights that help them improve their constituent relationships.

How do these six strategies impact sales success?

Sales is a numbers game in which luck and timing play significant roles. As Peter Thiel, cofounder of PayPal, says, "It is better to have great distribution than a great product."[2] Yet at the margin, presentation success is highly dependent on having customer insights to create proposals that are closely connected to the buyer's matter at hand and don't attempt to address or solve the wrong problem.

You can't be optimally persuasive by talking about yourself out of the context of how you address your customer's problems. You don't want to speak about anything you do without first having adequate knowledge about how it fits your customer's needs.

Verify your understanding of the customer's objectives upfront, without assuming you have them right. Adapt successfully to objections to inspire your client's confidence that your solution is the one that best suits your client.

The lack of soft skills is among the problems that create less-than-successful presentations. Three lecturers who teach an excellent course called Entrepreneurial Sales at MIT's Sloan School of Management (all of whom are themselves entrepreneurs) cite the failures to listen, adapt, and be confident as the most important reasons that salespeople fail.[3] Listening, adapting as needed, and inspiring confidence are among the essential soft skills for persuasive presentations. Practical approaches and techniques to enhance all of these are illustrated in the context of stories about the dynamics of the human interaction in actual sales presentations.

"Social skills are important in the modern labor market because computers are very poor at simulating human interaction ... adapting flexibly to changing circumstances. Such interaction is at the core of the human advantage over machines."

—David J. Deming, NBER Working Paper, 2015[4]

Do customers see these problems in presentations and do they matter?

A senior marketing executive at a chemicals company, Steve Bland, thinks so. By his own count Steve has attended over 30 sales and sales management seminars. Knowing your product stands out to him as an important trait of any successful salesperson, but so does the commitment to ask and listen. He told me a story about retaining a top customer who was annoyed by the approach taken by one of his salespeople. She was so upset with the salesperson for failing to ask about her concerns and listen to her before launching into his pitch that she vowed not to buy the company's products even if they were offered free of charge.

Relevance matters to this customer and many others in the business-to-business market. There are relevance voids in many sales presentations. A 2016 national survey by Gallup found a high level of dissatisfaction with sellers among B2B customers, so much so that 71 percent said they were considering taking their business elsewhere. These buyers felt that salespeople were too preoccupied with talking about product and price, and not focused on the fit with their customer's problems. Buyers want sellers who have insights into their customer's business needs and have custom-tailored approaches to satisfy them.[5]

A nationwide survey cosponsored by SalesForce.com found that business customers expressed a high level of appreciation for sales presentations that were "relevant and contextual," but felt that most presentations did not possess those qualities.[6]

Gallup followed their 2016 B2B survey with another one in 2017 that showed only "31 percent of buyers believe their suppliers understand their needs."[7]

When you consider anecdotes like those cited and the results of these research studies, you can see the need to close the relevance gap, and that there is an element of respect that customers look for in sales presentations as well. Customers don't want sellers to waste their time by failing to address the correct problem or talking about their impressive capabilities in ways that don't focus on customer needs. Buyers appreciate sellers who listen to them and don't assume that they know what their customers want.

Investment and other professional services presentations are not immune from these same criticisms. Individual investment clients see relevance gaps in the communications with their investment advisors. This customer comment reflects a typical sentiment, "Before you start explaining your economic outlook and investment process, ask me to tell you what is important to me about my portfolio."

Some wealth management firms have taken it upon themselves to comment on the seller—not client—orientation in their competitors' marketing efforts. On July 29, 2017, the Capital Group, Private Client Services, posted on its website, "It's amazing how many so-called wealth management firms spend most of their time talking about their investment products. But we begin the planning process, not by talking about products, but by understanding what you hope to accomplish with your life."[8]

This asset manager's observation can be corroborated by looking at some firms' public, client communications. As l looked through the website of a highly successful West Coast investment manager, I was amazed to see that a video about their separately managed account services hardly mentioned the customer. The informative video was about the organization and its investment approach, but there was no direct translation of what that information meant for the individual investor.

Another indicator of the validity of that conclusion is from my content analysis of actual, current new business presentations by two prominent, successful companies. The major shortcoming in otherwise very impressive documents was that the vast majority of pages talked about the seller's attributes without linking them to the customer needs they satisfied. The delivered presentations might have been different, but both written presentations cited multiple capabilities and credentials without making the customer connections.

Presentations that are more about the seller than the buyer are based on the view that the strength of the story will carry the day. They tend to address generic needs rather than being built from the ground up from a base of a well-understood and verified customer premise.

Of course, whether or not you focus on customer solutions, not just your organization's credentials, the real proof is in the execution. Every organization states its commitment to be customer-focused. Not every organization is committed to do what it takes to achieve that focus.

When you are in a sales role, your company will supply you with product knowledge and tell you how they want to be positioned in the marketplace. But knowing your customer and acting on that knowledge is up to you.

Customers buy from sellers they believe, trust... and like.

So, what about elements other than customer relevance? One famous, independent retailer in Texas, Jim "Mattress Mack" McIngvale, told me that successful salespeople are those that customers "believe, trust and . . . like." Mack lives by what he says. This person who calls himself part capitalist, part philanthropist, opened his furniture stores to evacuees from Houston's devastating Hurricane Harvey in 2017, another in a long list of community contributions that have endeared him to the people of Houston.

One of my lifelong friends and an accomplished architect, Mark Higgins, says that attracting customers "eventually comes down to whether they like you." And Robert Cialdini, the noted author on the subject of influence, considers likability to be one of the seven keys to being persuasive.[9] All these qualities were factors in my successful presentations.

The confidence and trust I inspired in one presentation to a major state government was the *only* aspect of that presentation that accounted for its success. I fostered that confidence by selling myself first on the match between what we offered and what the client needed most from its investment manager. Moreover, if that client hadn't liked me and my copresenter, we would have lost.

You earn and build trust by your actions. That means not making assertions that disagree with known facts. That means doing what you say you will do. Adhering to the expectations you create sounds pretty basic, but not doing so is one of the major reasons for losing an account—or worse, destroying an entire business.

Major corporations have collapsed simply because their senior management blatantly lost sight of what they promised their investors. They did things that they said they would not do. Once they did that, what they did afterward was almost immaterial. They had already lost their investors' trust and ownership stake in their company.

Is likability an innate quality? Is there any way to make a person who is not likable more likable? Anyone who asks and listens will be more likable (or at least less unlikable). Customers like salespeople who ask and listen to what is said.

Tactics for being insightful, relevant, confident, adaptable, and … liked are based on the key underpinnings of successfully persuasive presentations.

The following are key principles for persuasive presentations:

Presenters need faith in the fit.

Every presenter needs to know their product and believe in the fit between their products and the customer's matter at hand in order to inspire confidence in their customer. The best ways to foster that confidence are by selling yourself first and seeking inspiration from the people in your own organization who actually produce the products you sell. Those individuals are a great source for understanding the most meaningful ways to distinguish those products from your competition.

Creating a perfect product-client fit is the overarching goal; the firm that best achieves it wins.

There are many reasons why people buy. Rational economic motives tend to prevail. People buy mostly because they believe the seller's product best satisfies their matter at hand. Most people will give their brother-in-law's company a chance, but usually only as long they deliver the desired benefits at the right price.

Presenters need insights not just information to be successful in downstream marketing.

There is no better way to be comfortable and confident about what you are selling than to have true insights about what your client wants and needs. Conversely, the lack of such insights creates a cascade of problems for all downstream marketing efforts, wastes your own and your customer's time, and probably results in not making the sale.

Insights are different from information. An insight is a deeper and more accurate level of understanding—something that stands out, is notable, and cuts to the heart of the matter. If you want to be successfully persuasive, there is no substitute for going about the process of discovering insights and building your presentation around them.

The best way to discover insights is to ask open-ended questions and listen to the answers.

Insights come from interviewing your customer, key decision-maker, or influencer *before* you go into the meeting. Asking open-ended questions provides the uncommon richness of detail that you cannot uncover any other way, particularly when you are in the initial stages of understanding what your customers want, need, and look to you to provide.

Lay out the logic of your presentation upfront and verify that you are on the right course.

Asking for customer feedback about your understanding of their objectives, and your approach to meeting them at the start of your presentation will give you valuable—possibly game-changing—information. It is a good way to overcome the pitfalls of assuming. This is an active technique to obtain a consensus understanding when all influencers and decision-makers are in the room

Make constructive alterations as necessary to achieve the optimal product-customer fit.

Every presenter needs the right demeanor in countering objections, and the confidence that they can satisfy the client's matter at hand even as the client's parameters change. Soft/social skills play an important role in adapting successfully to the human buyer-seller interaction in the meeting room. Successful presenters are:

- Diplomatic, not defensive
- Constructive, not contentious

- ■ Consistent with known facts, and overall
- ■ Vigilant and flexible in adapting to changing circumstances

Much of presentation success has to with the dialogue in the conference room—not the prepared presentation itself—and how well the seller adapts to objections and new information.

Why it is worthwhile to invest time, resources, and energy to create and deliver persuasive presentations?

Selling is about persuasion. Everyone has the need to persuade others at one time or another—family, friends, employees, bosses, patients, and customers. In that sense everyone is in sales. Roseanne Bachman, the author of an excellent article on persuasion in the *Creighton University Magazine*, put it this way: "In a society where effectively persuading others can lead to increased sales, job promotions, social reform, and political office, skills that can increase widespread action are highly prized."[10]

If you work in any kind of marketing or sales role in investment management or financial services in general, you are likely to be reviewed and compensated based on your ability to attract and retain clients. But there is the career advancement dimension as well. When you make presentations, you make impressions on people who see you in action on a public stage. Presentations are sometimes auditions for roles that, unbeknownst to you, someone in a position of power is considering you to play.

You should not be looking for your next job when you make a presentation, but there might be something in what you say or do that ultimately leads to one. That was certainly the case for me. I made some pretty stark career transitions. I went from life as a marketing professor in two business schools, to a job with Young & Rubicam, a major New York advertising agency where I did research for consumer products like breath mints and household cleansers, to marketing and selling sophisticated investment products for Merrill Lynch (now a Bank of America company).

Presentation capability was one of the major reasons that Merrill Lynch hired me. I had no financial background or training when I started. Presentation success helped me survive and prosper when I got there. One of the reasons I have confidence in the presentation approach suggested here is because so many elements of that approach have worked for me.

When I joined the asset management group at Merrill Lynch, we had a very limited institutional presence. When I was given responsibility for institutional marketing, we began to develop relationships with some of the world's largest corporations, governmental entities, and affluent people. I was fortunate enough to establish or enhance relationships with clients like Coca-Cola, Wal-Mart, AT&T, Fiat-Chrysler, DuPont, Johnson & Johnson, the State of California, and IBM-United Kingdom, along with wealthy individuals and families. My perspective also has a lot to do with the effectiveness of the thirty talented investment management marketing professionals I was fortunate to manage at Merrill Lynch, who employed the proprietary presentation technology and approach we so successfully used to consistently produce a significant percentage of the net new mutual fund assets for the firm.

So this book offers my perspective on persuasive presentations, and I draw from the experience and expertise of senior managers in investment management and other businesses who loaned me some of their stories, along with a reality check on the applicability of the suggestions I make.

In her article on persuasion, Roseanne Bachman quotes Jennifer Metzler, a persuasion consultant to Fortune 500 companies, on why persuasive presenters are made, not born. "We may be hard-wired to want buy-in from others," she says, but "only through education and training do we develop the techniques to do it well."[11]

We can all benefit from new perspectives—even ones that seem to be a new take on an old idea—to get better at what we do.

CHAPTER 1

Never Assume

The success of all downstream marketing efforts depends on an insightful customer premise. Insights lead to a deeper and more accurate understanding of the customer. They are what stand out, are notable, and cut to the heart of the matter in a customer's decision-making process. Presenters have to resist the tendency to want to perfect what they say about their organization and its strengths before they have perfected their understanding of the customer. Reaching a level of understanding that constitutes insights about customers is not so easy, but it is necessary to be successfully persuasive.

The best, and only, way to obtain insights is to ask your customer the right kinds of open-ended questions and listen—and pay attention—to the answers. The best way to produce presentations that *don't* fit your client is to assume that what you *think you know* about your client is accurate. Assuming is never a good idea. Verifying your understanding always is a good idea.

I assumed I knew what my Australian billionaire client was looking for, and I got it wrong. The result was his complete rejection of our proposal. Before returning to that story, I want to say more about assuming and its unfailing ability to cause problems—even for the best and the brightest.

If I asked anyone in business whether they believed assuming was a bad idea, they would all say yes. Does that mean they don't fall victim to such mistakes? I doubt it. Jim Kennedy, my good friend and the former CEO of T. Rowe Price, told me this, "It is amazing to see many of the smartest and most talented people begin their explanations for why they made a mistake by saying the same two words: I assumed..."

The consequences of assuming range from the trivial to the titanic. Everyone can think of situations in their own lives and in history when bad decisions were made based on invalid assumptions.

This common flaw in decision-making continues to be exhibited in all echelons of society, business, and government. Presidents of the United States are not immune. One former president had to make a decision about dangerous adversaries who were responsible for the deaths of many Americans and others. The US military located the individuals and asked for permission from the president to capture or kill them.

The president gave the order and the operation proceeded. But it took place in the middle of a bustling city and several Americans were killed.

In a private conversation with an associate, the president remarked with regret, "I assumed they would take out the bad guys on an isolated road, not in a crowded marketplace."

Despite the fact that most everyone agrees that assuming is a bad idea, even the smartest people continue to make that mistake.

Now the rest of the story about the presentation in Australia...

Our billionaire client had just rejected our proposal, and I was not sure why.

I thought I clearly understood his objectives. I did not have any prior opportunity to meet with him. But my team had been given very clear directions about what he wanted from his forceful and opinionated CEO, and his CFO. I assumed—and therein lies the problem—that they were correct.

So why the instant "no"? The reason was just as our wealthy prospect said. My firm's proposal did not suit how *this man* wanted his money managed. In his mind, he had told us—that is, through his senior managers—what he expected. As far as he was concerned, we had our chance to produce an investment strategy that met those objectives, and we didn't deliver. What more was there for him to say? It was time to return to the polo field.

So what did I miss and how did I miss it? The view my team got from those chief lieutenants was not the view of the chief. What we later learned is that this client wanted an investment strategy with the potential to generate much higher returns than the one we suggested, and he was willing to take the added risk to achieve that.

The fact that his top managers relayed their boss's preferences incorrectly was not their problem, and it certainly wasn't their boss's problem. It was our problem. And once the boss said "no," any excuses were all water under the bridge.

This episode in our relationship showed that knowing the customer is fundamental. Yet it is hard to get right and so easy to get wrong. It is never wise to assume that what you think you know is accurate.

Customers buy when they believe that the seller's product best satisfies their particular matter at hand. The Australian business magnate was no exception. When you don't have a well-understood, insightful, and verified customer premise, you lack the foundation for successfully fitting your product to your customer. Sales and marketing failures don't get much more complicated than that.

I made the mistake of assuming in Australia. Now I had to overcome that mistake.

Our prospect was walking out of that room. It was a large room, but in a few seconds he would be out the door.

Before I tell you what I said in those moments before he left, let me add some context about my role in the interchanges. I was in Australia as a salesperson pursuing a sales opportunity. I was the director of Institutional Marketing for Merrill Lynch Asset Management (MLAM) that is now part of BlackRock. At the time, MLAM was one of the nation's largest asset managers. Merrill Lynch itself is now a Bank of America company. The business model for asset managers is in many ways very simple. It is all about attracting client assets and the fees they generate. The admirable mission is to help investors with their life and financial future.

When fulfilling that mission, supporting your business and employees requires money to manage, so you try to go to where the money is. It's rare to present your products and services directly to one of the wealthiest people in the world. Yet that was the opportunity I was given with this very wealthy Australian. And with that opportunity came a variety of pressures.

This billionaire was already an investment banking client at Merrill Lynch. An investment banker had asked my team to meet with this billionaire about managing a very large portfolio of his corporate and private assets. The cash portion of those assets had just grown substantially after the sale of several companies he owned.

Teamwork was one the five core principles of Merrill Lynch. Working together with others in the Merrill Lynch networks was essential to the growth of our investment management business, and a key to my personal success at the firm. The internal reputation of the asset management division as well my own standing would certainly be affected by how my team dealt with their billionaire client.

I may not have been expected to win his account. I certainly wanted to win it, but I was counted on to deliver a professional presentation that reflected well on asset management, and on Merrill Lynch.

At some point, every sales and marketing person is in a high-profile meeting with a demanding external audience. In that same room, there might be a watchful contingent of peers and senior management, assessing the way you handle yourself in representing your employer. Presentation success can have a big impact on sales results and on career advancement as well. At Merrill Lynch, the phrase, "Nothing succeeds like success," certainly held true.

This Australian corporate account would be one of the largest privately managed portfolios at the firm. It might not be the most significant or most profitable, but it would be among them. And it would help solidify the relationship of the company's principal shareholder with other parts of Merrill Lynch.

In any case, when you are in a production-driven firm in a production role, and you have the chance to manage money for one of the most affluent people in the world, you have to take advantage of it. As they say countless times in sports broadcasts, you have to make that pass, that catch, that tackle, that shot, or that putt. You get the point.

I arrived in Sydney on a bright summer morning with the head of our fixed income group and one of his portfolio managers. We headed to our client's corporate headquarters with Kevin, our investment banker in Australia, for some final briefings about his investment goals with his CEO, a man the business press dubbed Hacksaw Hal, and his CFO.

This was the first time we had met these people in person. Hal was a former slash-and-burn leveraged buyout artist, and the most authoritarian individual I had ever encountered. He was a controversial figure when we met him, and he later became a discredited executive who faced a flurry of charges in the United States for securities fraud. But we did not know that then. All we knew at that time was that Hacksaw Hal told us what his boss wanted and expected us to act on that guidance.

Hal informed us that the meeting with his boss would not be in the headquarters. Instead, we would shortly be taking the company helicopter to meet him at his ranch north of Sydney. The adventure continued with an enjoyable ride overlooking great views of lush countryside. I felt relaxed and enthusiastic about the presentation. It seemed that everything was on track and going well.

We touched down next to a large field with spectator seating and an outdoor café. This was a serious sports complex with a polo game in progress. One of the players was unmistakable—the Australian business mogul himself.

This was not a pickup game with local amateurs. He had invited two elite players from Argentina. These were "ten goalers," as they are called in polo. Fewer than ten players worldwide are given that rating. The mogul apparently felt that if he was going to play the game, it might as well be with the best players in the world. When he was not in Australia, he played in England. He typically rented an entire floor of the Savoy in London for himself and his entourage.

Some jobs, like mine with Young & Rubicam and with Merrill Lynch, give you a ticket to things you would otherwise never see. I grew up in Nebraska. We had cornfields, but no polo fields. While the business purpose was on my mind, this was one of those life experiences to appreciate.

The scene was my first indication of how this man chose to spend his money and live his life. He was an imposing figure, a larger-than-life individual who also lived large. Polo wasn't his only passionate pursuit. He was often called the world's greatest gambler because he won or lost $25 million in single sittings at the blackjack and baccarat tables in Las Vegas and London. But win or lose, he was likely to leave $1 million in the tip jar to be shared by the croupiers, dealers, cocktail waitresses, and other staff members whose help he appreciated. He was very definitive about how he wanted to spend his money and, as we soon discovered, how he wanted it invested as well.

When the polo match ended, he came directly to meet us in the living room of his ranch home. He glanced for no more than a few seconds at the presentation deck I gave him, then set it aside. I later learned that, like many successful people, he suffered from dyslexia and compensated for his difficulty with the printed word with a keen ability to listen.

I continued to explain our recommended approach to him without referring to the deck. He fully understood our suggested investment strategy before rejecting it with that one-sentence declaration: "This is not what I'm looking for."

After all that was involved in just getting to that point, it had taken mere minutes to go down in ignominious defeat. My colleagues were stunned by the quick dismissal. Meanwhile, Hal was uncharacteristically speechless, either mad that we'd wasted his time, entertained to see us flame out, or possibly both. The silence was deafening.

Our client was walking out of the room. No pleasantries were exchanged. He would be out the door in a few seconds. A lot flashed through my mind at that moment.

In those few seconds, as I faced the unpleasant prospect of failing to capitalize on a golden opportunity to manage money for one of the world's wealthiest people, I may have recalled the advice a senior executive gave me when I first joined Merrill Lynch, "Stay close to the revenue." (To survive and prosper you need to produce profitable revenue. In sales you are only as good as your last performance, and being able to close is critical.)

I certainly felt the disappointment of doing all that we had done just to get to this point only to fail. We came to Oz with what we thought he requested, only to be told by the Wizard that we should get ourselves back to Kansas.

I had to say or do something. This was not the way I wanted this odyssey to end. I said, "Sir, we can do better. We would like to come back tomorrow."

He stopped, looked back, and perhaps surprisingly, but certainly fortunately, said, "Yes, that would be fine."

A momentary reprieve! At that point, I had a hunch that we could still win his account. Some soft skills were involved here, or maybe it was just a lucky call on my part that manifested itself as a soft skill. Either way, the situation called for a human response not a programmed one. I made an admission that we had blown it, even though I wasn't sure why.

Our demanding billionaire said nothing about why he was unhappy with our proposal. That did not matter to me then, and had nothing to do with what I said. We could do no worse than we had already done. This was not the time to be defensive or cast blame, though we had good reasons to do so. We were given bad information from the CEO and CFO.

My demeanor in responding to rejection was one major reason this client gave us the second chance. Mine was a humble yet confident request. I really did believe we could do better, even though I may not have been sure how. This was a case of *how* you say it being more important than *what* you say. If I had not said what I said with conviction and diplomacy, I think we would have been finished. Clearly, if he had not liked me or my attitude, we would have been on our way home.

Another approach, the polar opposite of what I did at that moment, would have been to say and do nothing. I could have just watched our imposing client leave. He was a bit of an intimidating guy and he had said "no." Many salespeople in this situation would have just accepted his decision and taken the loss. And what then?

The sulking and recriminations would have begun and continued in the hotel bar. You might begin to blame yourself, then shift the blame to the client. You would lament the poor guidance you were given and complain about the instant rejection and lack of any specific reasons for it. You would tell yourself that the loss was clearly not your fault and get prepared to deliver that narrative to your bosses back at your ranch. But that is not the way to deal with adversity. It is analogous to being in a team meeting when there is a decision you don't like. Instead of arguing for your solution, you capitulate, go back to your office, shut the door, and complain about how you were right and the others on the team were misguided or failed to give proper attention to your opinion. Then continue with the carping to anyone who will listen to you. Yadda, yadda, yadda. You know this person and this behavior.

Though you may have the lone dissenting view, you have to try to do and say what you believe without being intimidated. Many bad life and business decisions might have been avoided if someone had just spoken up. Airplanes have crashed because airline crew members were so over-deferential (or maybe reverential) toward the pilot that they didn't press their case about really being out of fuel.

People in these situations speak up when they feel comfortable doing so, and they don't speak up as freely when they don't feel they can do so without being embarrassed, rejected, or ridiculed. That is one of the principal conclusions of an exhaustive study by Google on the performance of teams. That study showed that, more than anything else, the psychological safety of each member was critical to making teams work.[12]

When I said we could do better and would return with a revised proposal, I was speaking on behalf of our team. If I was unsure of the support I would receive in making any commitment, I would have deferred saying anything until I had the chance to confer with the other members. But there was no time to do that in the moment before the billionaire made his exit. Any discussion after that would have been too little too late.

Other members of my team could have spoken up. Maybe they deferred to me. I know they had never encountered a client situation like this one either. I was the lead presenter. If anything was going to be said, it was up to me to say it. I had to feel confident that whatever I said would be supported. From that perspective, I could say that I must have felt psychologically safe in making a commitment for the company when I said, "We can do better, and would like the chance to prove it."

There is a lesson here about not being frozen by rejection—having the confidence to speak up when it might be uncomfortable to do so. It also is a lesson on how to ask for a second chance. This is what salespeople mean when they say the sale starts when the client says "no."

Doing all of those things successfully requires soft and/or social skills that are not developed via artificial intelligence. But they can be enhanced by learning about the techniques that worked in situations like this one.

"Even with the most brilliantly trained minds, and most powerful technological tools, the greatest success comes from attending to human factors like leadership and soft skills."

—Scott Hartley[13]

So we survived to fight another day. We helicoptered back to Sydney for overnight talks with our headquarters in Princeton, New Jersey. The portfolio managers made their adjustments and we created a new presentation that was explicitly tied to our client's actual objectives. His CEO and CFO confirmed—and they were right this time—that he wanted a much more aggressive portfolio. That seemed to be in character. After all, this person was the world's greatest gambler.

When we arrived at the ranch the next morning, our client was back on the polo field with those world-class players from Argentina. The match was an interesting and entertaining prelude to our second-chance meeting.

I was very relaxed and optimistic that our second chance would work out.

The billionaire amateur polo player came straight from the match to meet us.

I began, but he immediately stopped me and asked, "Just what is it that you do?" with the tone of someone who wondered why I was even there in the first place.

Was this an indication that my instincts were wrong, and that we were poised for another fall? Maybe. He could have just been curious about my role. Still, I thought I knew what he was getting at, and that was: "Am I the salesperson?"

To some, sales and salespeople are all about unloading products. Countering these perceptions is an occupational hazard. But every business enterprise depends on sales to exist. Sales is not a tawdry profession; it is admirable one. There is nothing about being in sales that any salesperson should be defensive about. I wasn't happy about having my role and credibility questioned. But I needed an answer.

I gave him whatever impressive title I had at the time, but clarified that I was, in fact, a sales and marketing person.

"So," he said, "you're the one that flogs this stuff."

"Yes," I replied, "I'm the chief flogger."

My answer apparently passed muster with someone who'd made a considerable part of his fortune selling unglamorous products like want ads in his newspapers. He later told me that those small-space ads were "rivers of gold."

Having overcome that latest in a string of obstacles, I proceeded with the presentation. This was a verbal explanation on how we would tailor our resources to satisfy the bolder, more risk-tolerant investment objectives of someone who fit the profile of an original Australian business tycoon. We were going to give him the kind of exposure to the markets and potential returns that he had always intended.

Almost as quickly as he had rejected our first proposal, our mogul said yes to this one. The money was wired to us the next day. We had established one of the largest, privately managed accounts in the history of the firm. The investment banker was pleased with the result and the president of the asset management group was happy as well.

Note: This was not a case of telling this client what he wanted to hear and overpromising in the process. We had to be able to satisfy the expectations we agreed to. The only time we had a performance issue with this account was when one of the several portfolio man-

"If you want a friend, get a dog."

—Hacksaw Hal

Dealing with difficult clients can be part of the process. You can't sacrifice your corporate principles to satisfy them. The issue is how to deflect the blows and maintain the relationship. That particular challenge reached new heights for us with Hacksaw Hal. He was as much our client as the man he worked for. We could not ignore Hal's input. He was definitive about what he and his boss wanted. That was his personal style.

Hal was a singular character in the annals of business. He became that discredited executive after he left his job with the Australian conglomerate, but he was a major part of the story while he was there.

Hal's style was intimidation and confrontation. I once brought him to Merrill Lynch's New York headquarters to meet the CEO. It was a way, I thought, to thank a new major client and find ways to build on the relationship with his various companies.

Hal had a different agenda. He wanted special concessions. "That would be unfair to our other clients," our CEO said. That answer was not good enough for Hal. The friendly conversation degenerated into a fist-pounding-on-the-conference-room-table shouting match.

Hal's anger at not getting his way boiled over. He escalated the already heated dialogue by calling Merrill Lynch's senior managers the most incompetent people he had ever dealt with. I don't think he considered me to be in that group, but I wasn't sure.

Hal told Merrill's CEO that he could call any firm on Wall Street and they would jump through hoops to have this account. Our CEO's Irish temper flared. He went to his desk, and shot back, "Go ahead, here's the phone," and slammed it down on the desk.

So much for friendly relationship-building!

Eventually, the meeting concluded with him offering an olive branch by saying sincerely, "Good-bye and good luck."

"Luck's got nothing to do with it," Hal shot back, storming out of the office.

Fittingly, the son of the cofounder of Merrill Lynch, Pierce, Fenner & Smith (and the director of the firm's international division) witnessed the entire episode. He told me later that he'd never experienced—or even heard about—an argument like that one in his entire career at the firm. He cited the incident in many public speeches after that as a clear example of how Merrill Lynch would never sacrifice its principles to bow to the demands of an unreasonable client.

As it turned out, Hal was the one who left the Australian billionaire and his company. But the account stayed with us.

I had managed to get along with Hal despite his abrasive, over-the-top style—I had to. But, as he frequently told me, "If you want a friend, get a dog."

agers eventually assigned to it simply took it upon himself to not adhere to the investment strategy we had agreed to execute. He took less risk than this client wanted. In this case, the returns suffered. If he had done what the client counted on and performed poorly that would have been another matter. In this case, the client was unhappy and the portfolio manager was removed from the account. Like most institutional clients, this one expected us to maintain the investment discipline we agreed to. Whether you gain more or lose less by not following what your customer is paying you to do is beside the point. You will lose their trust and the account as well.

From the moment he said yes to our revised proposal, I had a very good relationship with the Australian business baron. He hosted a dinner a few months later in his country home outside of London with the chairman of Merrill Lynch, the head of the asset management group, and me. He later asked us to pursue joint ventures with him in Australia. It was quite a turnaround.

I had continued to earn the confidence of my bosses in my ability to handle high-profile situations like this one. I was given broad responsibility, and a great deal of autonomy for managing our marketing efforts. Presentation success in this case had, from a shaky start, produced sales success and career success as well.

I don't want to overanalyze the presentation in Australia, but it was worth dissecting because of what it taught me about the need to create proposals that fit the client, about the difference between insights and information, and the pitfalls of assuming. It suggests techniques and a posture for adjusting and responding to serious objections, the vital role of confidence, and how to inspire it in your audience.

Conclusions and implications

Deliver an initial proposal that fits.

The reason we failed in our initial presentation is that we delivered a proposal that did not meet the needs of our client. It required major alterations. If we had been on target the first time, we could have made minor changes and won the account right there and then. You need to know enough about your client to create an initial proposal that keeps you in the game.

This story showed how hard it is to modify a proposal that is not even reasonably relevant. We created more work for the client, strained his patience and, rather than let us make major alterations on the spot, he just said "no."

The solution is to make greater efforts to confirm the client's objectives by being more persistent in asking follow-up questions when you interview them and/or anyone who speaks for them.

Double down on your effort to have insightful knowledge of the customer.

This experience demonstrates that the task of knowing the customer is not elementary, even when already exercising seemingly proper due diligence. The billionaire was the real and only decision-maker. I had never met him before the meeting. But I should have tactfully verified my understanding of his objectives when we did meet, and not assumed that what I had learned from his senior managers was correct. The episode showed the difference between information and insights. Information was in the briefing from the CEO and CFO. The insight was what the principal owner really wanted in his portfolio without a filter from those individuals. The only way to uncover that insight was by asking.

Don't assume. Verify.

What might I have said to tactfully confirm my understanding with the billionaire himself? Something like this: "This is our understanding of your investment objectives. Did we miss anything? Is there anything else you want us to know or be sure to discuss?"

These questions elicit new material information that can change the course of a presentation. When asking these questions, be careful not to imply that the people who briefed you were incorrect or suggest that you are questioning what they said. Asking, "Did *we* miss anything?" shifts the focus away from them to your interpretation of what they said. But it still accomplishes your goal of getting feedback on your approach before you start your presentation.

These are great questions to ask almost any audience in almost any presentation. If you've never incorporated such questions into your opening remarks, here's why you should: If the audience confirms that you're on the right track, you can proceed with some degree of confidence that you're addressing the key issues they want to address. On the other hand, if they add something else or correct your understanding, you have a chance to refocus your presentation before you get too far into solving what may be the wrong problem.

Asking these questions over repeated occasions will produce new material information, uncover blind spots, and possibly, game-changing insights. This is more than "tell 'em what you're gonna tell 'em." It is confirming—not assuming—that you are on the right track.

Selling can restart when the client says no.

What else could I have said or done as our client was leaving the room? I could have asked him to stop to clarify what was wrong with our proposal. However, why we lost was not critical at that point anyway. What good would have come from asking him to give us a debriefing on what we missed? He had just said "no," and we were going to find out why from his senior managers.

I could have asked him whether there was something we could do to change his mind. Sounds reasonable. But why didn't we deliver a relevant proposal while we had the chance? Besides, that would seem like the approach of a new car salesperson to keep a customer from leaving the showroom. This individual was not looking for a better price or a complimentary options package.

I could have said nothing and taken up the matter later with the CEO and CFO. But that would have been asking them for the second chance that they lacked the authority to give me. Plus, they had already misled us once. Why would I count on them now? This was something that required going around the chain of command to the client himself.

Saying, "We can do better. We would like to come back tomorrow," was the best and right thing to say, and to say to the person directly. (It was the right thing because it worked.)

Prepare to think on your feet.

The obvious tipping point that gave us the chance to win the account was saying, "We can do better," and asking for the second chance. With that think-on-your-feet tactical response, I was able to generate moxie at the right time—mostly because I was sold on my firm's ability to satisfy this particular client's unique objectives. Actually, I had no choice but to take that confident stance. A statement like that, without conviction, would have been worthless.

These may be soft skills, but they are critical skills in persuasive communications, and they can be learned by understanding what worked to save accounts like this one. You could characterize what I said and did as a technique to respond when you have a deal-killing flaw in a presentation that was your mistake. Provide a human response, concede that you were on the wrong track, and ask for a moment to regroup and get back on the right one.

Lean on your confidence in the customer fit.

Another technique for successfully adapting is to lean on your confidence in your ability to satisfy your customer's problem; use it as a beacon to guide you.

In my case, this was drawing from a well of justifiable confidence when I needed it most. Our firm was a major player for the kind of portfolio this client wanted and needed. I was successful in persuading him that it was worth his time to give a firm with our resources and expertise a second chance.

This experience illustrates why confidence is such an important element in successful presentations. It may be the most important aspect in differentiating one presenter and organization from another. Confidence is not an innate skill, but it can be learned and enhanced for each specific situation.

Based on what I said and how I said it, this billionaire thought we *could* do better and that it was worth his time to listen. A confident request inspired a confident response. Don't waver. If you express any doubt, you will usually lose by default anyway.

Tenacity helps.

As Winston Churchill said, "Never, never give up." There is no proposal that does not require alterations to succeed. That is the mindset for clearing the most serious hurdles in any meeting. Confidence and determination can turn an ill-fitting proposal into one perfectly suited to your client.

Don't consider case histories to be one-off examples.

I was recently back in Australia with my daughter and, while there, we visited the T. Rowe Price office in Sydney. She knew the billionaire story and thought the person at T. Rowe Price might want to hear it.

He was amazed that, with all of the major banks and money managers in that country, people from a firm in the United States were able to land a huge account with such a prominent Australian business titan.

It *is* a great story that has useful implications for any presenter. And as it turned out, it was not a once-in-a-lifetime situation for me. In fact, what happened in dealing with that client had a direct influence on how I dealt with a proposal-killing response from another customer who would have a major long-term impact on our assets and fees. When I got to that point in the meeting with that client, it was déjà vu all over again.

CHAPTER 2

Always Verify

A ssuming can get you into trouble. It got me into trouble in Australia, but there was also a clear benefit from that experience. I was better prepared to deal with a challenge that had many parallels to the one we faced in Australia.

A new client fired an opening salvo during a presentation that took place just two miles from George Washington's Revolutionary War headquarters in Morristown, New Jersey. The client was a Fortune 500 company in the telecommunications industry. The presentation was a proposal to administer and provide investment funds for the company's employee retirement program. The competition included the country's top asset managers.

If you are someone who enjoys being in the fray—and you are measured and rewarded for winning—this was just the kind of pitch you want to be in. The plan had significant assets, as well as the prospect of strong and profitable growth. It was a major opportunity to establish a relationship with a prominent and prestigious client.

"Declaring that you know the customer's perspective without engaging them is foolish and will get you into trouble."

—Jonathan Horowitz, Citrusbyte[14]

I began this meeting by doing what I did not do at the beginning of the presentation in Australia. I did not assume what the client expected. I asked them to confirm that my understanding was correct. The question I asked was essentially this one: "This is our understanding of your objectives and how we plan to address them. Is there anything we missed that you want us to be sure to cover?"

One person answered, and she was the CEO. "Yes," she said, "There is something. We have all heard that your investment performance is not very good."

It was a completely unanticipated severe criticism—and a seemingly terminal diagnosis of the suitability of our mutual funds for her company's needs.

As was the case in the "land down under," this presentation seemed to fail almost immediately after it started.

The CEO's answer to my verification question, and what it put into motion, epitomizes why the quest for insights should continue right up to the start of your presentation.

Why? You may believe that you fully understand the client's specific objectives going into the meeting. You may feel that the RFP clearly laid them out. You may be completely confident prior to the presentation that you have a proposal that satisfies those objectives.

But assuming, as we've seen, is not a sound business strategy. Having a research mindset is. It reminds you to ask for directions, especially when you're not sure where you're going or how best to get there.

Even when you have done client interviews before the meeting, asking the opening verification questions is still worthwhile because it gives you one last, best chance to gain collective feedback on your

---

Why verify?

- ✔ Gain consensus when all players are in the room
- ✔ Discover game-changing insights that put you on a more correct course
- ✔ Uncover blind spots
- ✔ Customers appreciate your effort to get it right before launching into your pitch

intended direction for the meeting and avoid potential blind spots.

The question I asked the client in Morristown accomplished that exactly. It gave me the consensus view of the customer and the key decision-makers. It was a view that could not have been obtained in any way that did not involve having all of them in the room at the same time—a below-the-surface discovery that shaped the rest of that meeting in completely unforeseen ways.

We were making a proposal for administering a defined contribution plan that bundled investments with many other services. The CEO's criticism of our investment performance threatened to jeopardize the total team effort.

Others from Merrill Lynch who were in the room thought—justifiably so—that the CEO's perception of our fund performance had, on its own, put us in danger of losing the account.

I didn't have to guess what Roger, my senior management counterpart in the room, was thinking. I knew it was this: "Asset Management just blew this deal for all of us."

Like me, Roger was paid to deliver results. Unlike me, his management reminded him of that every day. Given his internal demands, I took it as compliment that whenever Merrill Lynch had an opportunity to present our services to a major client, Roger wanted me involved. Working together, we were successful in establishing relationships with some of the largest and most prominent retirement plans in the United States. But this client account did not seem likely to be another one of those success stories.

However, there was a positive outcome from asking that opening question. I now had a clear idea what the group in the room needed to hear from me. Their question was simply, "Why should we select funds from a firm that we believe has an inferior track record?"

I needed an answer that proved we had specific funds that could provide the level of investment performance the client expected. I needed to change the CEO's perception that none of our funds were competitive. I had to convince the CEO and the committee that using our funds would not make them look bad to other managers in the company or their employees. Clearly, no one wanted to disadvantage their employees' retirement accounts with investments that performed poorly. I had to prove that would not be the case.

Even CEOs have fears about making bad decisions.

There was no timeout to regroup in response to what the CEO had just said. I had to adapt on the fly. But a few principles guided me and can guide anyone when dealing with serious customer objections.

Don't argue with your client. From their point of view, they are almost always right.

The CEO's assessment of our investment performance was correct in one respect. As a fund family, our returns lagged those of our major competitors, particularly in the equity funds category. There was no point in disputing her assessment. If she had leveled a charge that was obviously false, yes. But on this point she was mostly correct in her view. Also true was that we managed certain individual mutual funds that were very strong performers.

Acknowledge the customer's point of view, but diplomatically set the record straight.

I acknowledged that the CE0's blanket perception was valid. I essentially told her that she was right, but I believed the investment choices I was about to recommend were not poor performers, but actually some of the best in their respective asset classes, and that I felt confident that after my presentation she would agree. I then proceeded to give her the relevant evidence to support that claim.

Never try to stretch the facts to counter criticism.

If I had tried to dispute the CEO's characterization, I would have lost all credibility. She knew the facts about our overall fund performance in the equity funds category. Had I proceeded to say something in conflict with those facts, our presentation would have ended right there.

Our overall equity funds performance did have its weaknesses, but the array of investment products I had selected for this plan did not include a single one with a less-than-competitive record. Fortunately, we had just enough top-performing funds to help me confidently and credibly make my case.

Complete transparency versus competitors' products

How did I make the performance case for our funds?

I showed the performance of our funds against category averages and market indexes, and also against specific alternatives from prominent investment managers. These were the individual mutual funds that I knew—or thought I knew—to be in contention for this assignment. They included some funds from competitors that would have been considered peers of our funds. This was exactly the kind of performance analysis called for. Without the head-to-head comparisons, the client could still question whether our performance was in line with that of funds from asset managers like Fidelity, Vanguard, T. Rowe Price, and American Funds. I would have been less persuasive with this client and many others without these transparent peer group comparisons.

Most every fund I recommended offered performance and other attributes that were at parity with—or superior to—competing funds, some of which were managed by the other firms who sat in the waiting room. I was fortunate to have one fund that was such a peerless, superior performer in its category that it created a halo effect for every other investment option I suggested. It was the Merrill Lynch Global Allocation Fund.

There are about nine thousand registered mutual funds in the United States. They cover every asset class—domestic and international, and most every investment style conceivable. There are few, if any, truly unique mutual funds. But Global Allocation was close to it. It's still in existence, but now it's part of BlackRock. With over $40 billion in assets, BlackRock Global Allocation is one of the largest mutual funds in the country.

The distinctive aspect of this fund is that it invests in stocks and bonds both within and outside of the United States. The fund's historical custom benchmark is 60 percent stocks and 40 percent bonds, and 60 percent of the investments in those asset classes were in the US and 40 percent outside the US. With this broad mandate, it's a very difficult fund to manage. Essentially, the fund is able to access almost the entire investment universe.

This fund had many attributes of particular relevance to defined contribution plan sponsors. One was, since its inception, the fund was managed by two of the most talented and capable portfolio managers at Merrill Lynch, with help from a group of top-performing equity fund managers in specific regions of the world, such as Europe and the Pacific Rim. It was an all-star team in every good sense of the term. One of those managers remained as a senior portfolio manager on the fund along with fifty individual investment professionals.

The fund's mandate, coupled with this portfolio management expertise, positioned it to satisfy a variety of investor objectives. For some, it met their need for a lower volatility, foundation fund, which could be augmented with more narrowly defined investments. For other clients, it was a way to get global exposure in stocks and bonds.

Some investors liked the fund for its downside protection. As the portfolio managers told me in our many conversations, the fund would almost certainly lag broad-based, all-equity funds in bull markets, but would remain more buoyant in bear markets. In fact Global Allocation, as of 2017, still has the rare distinction of providing the investment equivalent of the "free lunch." It has produced higher returns than a composite of world stocks, with one-third less volatility.[15]

When it comes to selling yourself first, this kind of input from the people who actually produce what you are selling is very beneficial. I always felt more confident after talking to our portfolio managers. They consistently gave me ideas about the meaningful distinctions of their funds for our clients. In the case of Global Allocation, I had the leading global, multi-asset fund in the industry to offer to our clients. It had the most impressive team of managers and the best risk-return profile in its category. And that last attribute made it the ideal all-season fund that any retirement plan investor would want as the bedrock of their portfolio.

The facts about this basically bulletproof fund stood in strikingly stark contrast to the telecommunications client's opinion about our overall fund performance. I know that this single investment option caused them, along with countless other clients, to have a more positive opinion of our entire fund family.

Comparing the Global Allocation Fund to peers and benchmarks was easy. It had no peers and exceeded all benchmarks. I made that point very clearly, and I know it resonated with the CEO in Morristown. I needed a fund like that to counter her negative perception of our fund family.

Basking in the halo of a superior product is an approach not lost on any marketing person. I went beyond touting the advantage to pressing it. I approached this the way I play poker. I am a respectable poker player. I am not good at bluffing. Other players catch on to my strategy pretty quickly. I have only one strategy, and that is: when I have a strong hand, I play it. I call and keep raising, welcoming anyone to challenge and call and raise again. Yet I did that only when I had a virtually unbeatable hand. That was the kind of hand I was dealt with the Global Allocation Fund, and how I played it. I was supremely confident in this fund and its fit with many clients. That confidence inspired confidence in my clients. The implicit and probably the explicit message I tried to deliver was that, if a customer selected us, they would be getting the premier fund in a category particularly important to their retirement plan participants.

The keys to altering this client's negative perceptions were the exceptional relevant strengths of Global Allocation as well as the peer group investment performance of the other funds I was suggesting.

In an era of instant evaluations of everything and everyone, if you don't tell your customers how you stack up against other competitors, someone else will. One of the reasons I preferred to show our performance versus competitors was to control the dialogue, and even inoculate the customer against negative commentary from a third party. I knew that we had a credibility gap and this was a way to fill it.

Pension consultants or other fund managers would likely weigh in. In fact, those third parties may have been responsible for the CEO's negative impressions of our products.

If you are proposing a fund or a group of funds to a client, you will be more persuasive when you show how they perform against their competitors, not just category averages. I think that is particularly true when competing to replace existing funds in a plan, such as would be the case with defined contribution investment-only proposals.

What I didn't know at the start of the meeting when the CEO raised her objection was that I would so clearly need those head-to-head comparisons—along with the Global Allocation Fund—to move our funds back into contention for any possible consideration by this client. I knew more about the strengths of our products than anyone outside of my firm. And I had the facts clearly displayed for the client to support my assertions.

My confidence in our products and their fit with the plan sponsor and their employees had to shine through. As long as I was perceived as honest, even claims that ran counter to the customer's initial impressions would likely be accepted.

The known fact was our relative weakness in overall equity fund performance. The unknown-to-the-client, but true, fact was the excellent performance of the specific mutual funds I was recommending for their plan. I said everything I said with a high degree of conviction, and backed it up with factual evidence.

As it turned out, I may have given the CEO and her committee more supporting and relevant data about our performance versus competing funds than our competitors did about theirs. I got valuable information from her answer to my opening verification question and made significant alterations in the tone and content of my presentation as a result. I was justifiably confident and it showed.

The next day, we learned that we'd won the account. All of the funds I recommended were included in the company's plan.

The takeaway: Asking and not assuming can yield game-changing results.

I don't know whether or not what I presented shocked the CEO and her committee as it was at such odds with their perceptions of our fund performance. They may have given me credit for absorbing the blow and continuing on unfazed by their challenge. But in the end, they had to be convinced by the strength of the evidence that our funds would be an excellent fit with the kind of investment menu they wanted for their employees. The comparative performance and other data I presented allowed them to suspend their disbelief in the quality of our funds and reverse their preconceived notions.

The moral of the story is that I would certainly have failed if I had not had the opportunity to confront the unknown biases against our funds right away, up front. The question I asked at the outset produced an absolutely game-changing insight.

Without that insight, I would not have spoken with as much conviction about our competitive performance. I was up against the wall. It was not a time for a timid response.

But the situation also called for a bit of humility, respect for the client's point of view, and a positive attitude. It was time to be constructive not contentious. A "you're wrong, we're right and here's why" approach would not have worked in this case, or maybe in any case.

Every presenter should begin their presentation by laying out the logic of their presentation and then asking questions, like these: "This is our understanding of your objectives and how we plan to address them. Have we missed anything? Is there anything else you want us to be sure to cover?"

Asking these questions is no substitute for interviewing the client—preferably in person—well before you walk into the meeting room. Once you get there, however, it is vitally important to confirm what you think you learned in those conversations. I can't imagine how doing so would not be helpful for any persuasive presentation made by any seller for any product.

When faced with a serious challenge, stay positive and stick to the facts.

✔ When a customer raises objections, don't feel insulted.

✔ Always be constructive, never contentious. Listen carefully, acknowledge their point of view, and diplomatically state yours. You might say, for example, "I understand your point and how you reached it, but here are some facts that suggest a more positive conclusion."

✔ Clearly, you don't want to let an obviously false negative perception stand, but even then your response must be diplomatic and respectful.

✔ Be totally transparent. Address their concerns by showing the negatives that they've mentioned in bold relief. That will give you more credibility when you highlight the positives.

✔ Let your data speak for itself. Stick to stating facts.

✔ Never stretch the truth. Contradicting known facts will catch up with you and all of your credibility will be lost.

✔ Be enthusiastic about the chance to respond to objections. If there are no questions or challenges to your proposition, the client may have already made their decision. Questions mean you're still in the game.

✔ A positive attitude can only help. A defensive posture will only hurt your chances and probably be fatal.

✔ Remember: you can still make modifications to what you're proposing, even in the sales meeting. Remain flexible. You're not there to deliver a recommendation that is not able to be altered for a better fit.

It is impossible to anticipate what a buyer may have read about your company on social media or learned through word of mouth or other third party. Negative comments from unknown sources are the kind of blind spot I encountered in the meeting in New Jersey. Any presenter could face a similar situation. Asking whether there is anything else the customer wants you to discuss is one way to bring those issues to the surface and give you an opportunity to address them, particularly when there are baseless charges made by unreasonable or disgruntled customers.

This suggestion to seek clarification up front and probe for other issues that may be of concern to the customer may be the single most important and usable idea for any presenter.

The ability to adapt is a necessity in being persuasive. Invest in learning about new techniques and the best practices for doing that. Your incentive is that you don't want to be one of those salespeople who fails specifically because of an inability to make the alterations necessary to suit the changing circumstances and new client information that surfaces in every meeting.

CHAPTER 3

Be Insightful Not Just Informed

You might think that clients will tell you what is most important to them in the RFP, or what some in engineering call the Notice of Opportunity.

In Australia, I was given the background and assignment information directly from the client's CEO and CFO. In the case of the telecommunications company in New Jersey, I had their detailed RFP. Both of those sources of information either turned out to be inaccurate or lacked a critical insight about something that would ultimately determine the outcome.

So what *can* you take away from assignment information that is contained in these printed documents? Obviously, pay close attention and respond exactly to what the customer asks for. As any proposal writer knows, if you don't adhere to each specific request for information, you will likely be disqualified early on.

But let's say you have done that. Consider what my good friend, engineer and successful commercial builder, John Ryan, told me about the effort necessary to know your customer: "If everything you know is what's in the RFP, you've already lost."[16]

Why did John say that? Because client-issued assignment materials, such as RFPs, never tell the entire story. Information about every customer—and what they want in a product or a vendor—can't be found in those documents alone. Public documents don't give you the *story behind the story*. They fail to address the subtleties of the decision-making process. They exclude information issuers don't want to put in writing, and probably don't illuminate the perspectives of key decision-makers.

For example, what you might want to know, and might not find in the RFP, is why the previous vendor is being replaced. Obviously, you want to avoid the mistakes that vendor made, and the only way to do that is to know what those mistakes were.

Similarly, documents like RFPs rarely contain any ingoing biases against your organization, much less the reasons for those perceptions. There was nothing in the RFP about the objection I encountered in the presentation to the telecommunications company in New Jersey.

You can't obtain that information without knowing and talking to the client before you go in. What's more, as every institutional salesperson knows, most important business decisions are made by multiple decision-makers and influencers—some of whom you may never get a chance to speak with before the meeting. Selecting a new pension fund manager or an array of funds for a defined contribution plan certainly falls into the category of decisions by committee. While this not breaking news, presenters for institutional asset management services simply have to understand the multiple and varied perspectives of decision-makers in the room during the presentation.

No one can know all the people and perspectives involved in an organizational sale. But you have to make the effort to know the major ones. If you're planning to present your IPO (initial public offering) or other funding request to a mutual fund manager, for example, value and growth managers and those using other investment styles will be in the room together. They each have particular goals regarding what they want to hear from you. They look at the same investment in terms of whether or not it meets their particular investment screens.

Going into the meeting with a one-size-fits-all approach may end up not addressing the concerns implied by either management style. You must understand the criteria that subgroups in the audience will use, and provide your view as to how your stock or company matches up.

The information you really need can only be gained by speaking with the client directly, and listening. Insights about the perspectives of multiple influencers are found via interviews and virtually nowhere else.

Rustling the Merrill Lynch bull away from its owner

Let's look at an example of material information integral to the success of a presentation that would not be in a public document. The client was Merrill Lynch. The opportunity was to be their new advertising agency. Young & Rubicam New York, now Y&R New York, was one of the contenders invited to make their pitch. Merrill Lynch, now a Bank of America company, has been a Wall Street institution for decades. It is one of the largest retail and capital markets financial services firms in the nation. It was known as "The firm that brought Wall Street to Main Street." Merrill Lynch earned that reputation with its commitment to the interests of the individual client, and to providing investor education. It became the dominant retail brokerage firm of the '40s, '50s, and '60s, and is still one of the dominant firms.

The founders of Merrill Lynch lived through crises in the financial markets, but were known as people who saw opportunity in the long term for their clients and their firm. That positive outlook on investing and on the United States as a country was emblematic of the culture of the firm throughout its history, and it remains that way.

That attitude was vividly and creatively displayed in one of the most famous television commercials ever made for a financial services firm. The commercial featured wonderful cinematography of a bull running with a beautiful backdrop of a scene from the American West. That tag line was simply: "Merrill Lynch is Bullish on America."

Merrill Lynch's advertising agency created the slogan that epitomized what Merrill Lynch wanted to mean to investors and their financial future. The agency that made that great commercial and wrote that tag line was Ogilvy & Mather.

Merrill Lynch uses a similar sentiment in its current advertising: "At Merrill Lynch we're bullish on the future. Yours." But the Merrill Lynch account with Ogilvy was abruptly terminated and put up for bid. Madison Avenue agencies lined up to pitch the account of one of the most well-known financial services firms in the United States.

Why would Merrill Lynch fire an agency that had created one of the most iconic commercials and slogans in advertising history?

The reported reason was that Ogilvy made the fatal mistake of selecting one of Merrill Lynch's arch-rivals to handle Ogilvy's IPO. This
information, one of the primary drivers behind Merrill Lynch's decision to bid out their account, definitely was not contained in the RFP
issued by Merrill Lynch. But the seriousness of the slight was indeed a
key factor in Merrill Lynch's decision to drop Ogilvy, and it set a standard that they would apply to any future vendor.

There may have been other reasons for the change. In any case,
those issues would not likely have been part of the RFP. RFPs are
typically not forums for criticizing suppliers, professional services
providers, and other vendors. They are straightforward, boilerplate
documents that outline business needs, and establish a framework for
competitive bids.

That said, it was very important to know why Ogilvy had been
fired, and what it was about their advertising that was not of concern—and liked. Y&R learned that Merrill Lynch was happy with the
Bullish on America campaign.

More important was determining that the Merrill Lynch bull itself
was not the guilty party in the firing of their predecessor. That was an
important client insight, because it paved the way for Y&R to retain
the now-famous Merrill Lynch bull and the brand awareness and imagery it had built. Y&R would be able to take advantage of what the
bull symbolized—the confident, capable services offered by Merrill
Lynch. The bull could remain a signature element in any advertising
Y&R proposed. And it was.

Y&R was able to follow a tough act by creating another classic
campaign. In one of the most memorable, award-winning commercials Y&R ever produced, the still famous, and real Merrill Lynch bull
delicately maneuvers through a china shop, between shelves of actual
Baccarat crystal and Wedgwood plates. The bull completed the course
flawlessly and did not even tip any of the pieces. (But a set designer
apparently did—dropping a $3,500 candelabra during the staging).

Another commercial showed the bull solving a maze cut through
a field of corn. The imagery in both commercials dramatically commu-
nicated the value of a positive outlook and a superior and deft capa-

bility to guide investors in the difficult-to-navigate investment world. The new tag line at the end of those terrific commercials was: "Merrill Lynch: A Breed Apart."

I wish I could have been involved in the development of that creative strategy and those commercials. I was not. By the time I joined Y&R, the agency had already won the Merrill Lynch account. Yet Merrill Lynch's switch to Y&R did prove life-changing for me. While at Y&R, I was assigned to the Merrill Lynch account. Coincidentally, that account loss for Ogilvy—and the win for Y&R—was what put me in a position that led to a job offer from Merrill Lynch, and a great and very fortunate career run there.

Back to the matter at hand: The moral of the rest of story centers on uncovering insightful knowledge about your audience—things that are not entirely obvious on the surface in client commentary or client documents. Many decision-significant issues lurk below. As always, the best way to learn about them is to ask your customer directly to tell you what they are.

There is an enormous amount of data on many customers today—big data, syndicated and proprietary research, customer relationship management (CRM) data bases, and so forth. Anyone can "get smarter" with this information. But assuming that information is sufficient, relevant, or even accurate is not a good idea. It certainly cannot provide the level of insightful knowledge necessary to effectively tailor what many financial services and other firms can offer to many of their customers—and it certainly can't help the average seller become the kind of trusted advisor that these buyers want.

In her recent TED Talk, "The human insights missing from big data," Tricia Wang suggested that data science injects what she calls a "quantification bias" into the use and interpretation of data.[17] People with this view tend to want only the immediately measurable. What they miss is what can be found in client interviews. Interviews based on small sample sizes, Wang suggests, "can deliver incredible depth and meaning." Even in a digital world, face-to-face interaction and the dialogue it produces, is still an essential source of customer knowledge.

Incredibly, despite the fact that "know your customer" is an admonition that virtually every seller must follow, not knowing the audience may be the single biggest reason for less-than-effective presentations. Part of the reason for that is that knowing the audience in industries like investment management is hard to get right/easy to get wrong. It requires curiosity, diligence, and a search for insights, *not just information.*

What are insights?

What do I mean by insights? How do insights differ from information?

The *Oxford American Dictionary* defines an insight as a "deeper and more accurate level of understanding of a person, their beliefs and their motivations." Insights differ from information. Insights are what is salient—i.e. notable, stand out, or are mission critical. Insights are the heart of the matter at hand. Insights are multidimensional, not superficial. They have a degree of richness not available in more categorical responses.

"Our cows won't wait three days for power to be restored" is a real comment from the owner of major cheese producer. His remark conveyed a key requirement for an off-the-grid power generation system his company was considering. Their need for reliability and outage scheduling for this equipment was illustrated in rich and meaningful terms.

This insight is a good example of the value of asking open-ended questions and listening. The effect of a power supply breakdown on this milk processor was an actionable comment that would not have been uncovered in any other way. The manufacturer devised multiple means of reducing the odds of more than twenty-four hours of downtime in their power system.

Insights like this one are about what Simon Sinek calls the "Why."[18] If you know not only what is important to your customers, but *why* those things are important, you will be in much better position to address their true needs and, in the process, set yourself apart from your competition.

Double down on your efforts to discover insights.

When you don't have insights, you can ...

✔ solve the wrong problem.
✔ lose the opportunity to show how you can address the correct problem.
✔ have a less focused meeting because you have to adjust and accommodate for your lack of relevant information.
✔ annoy your prospective client because you assumed— incorrectly—that you knew what they wanted and needed.
✔ only speak about what is generically good about your product.
✔ lose the account.

When you do have insights, you can ...

✔ address the things you do that relate specifically to your buyer's matter at hand.
✔ be more confident that what you say is relevant. Relevance matters.
✔ foster credibility and trust because you made the effort to listen and learn.
✔ have a better chance of winning against other similarly capable and informed competitors.
✔ have clues about how to add value to your client's business.
✔ uncover blind spots that can redirect your presentation and make it a better fit with newly discovered customer objectives.

You have a lot to lose when you don't have insights, and a lot to gain when you do.

Insights are irreplaceable

- ✔ Foundation for all down-stream marketing success
- ✔ Notable, at the-heart-of-the-matter, mission-critical for the client
- ✔ Not in big data, CRM profiles, RFPs or boilerplate categories
- ✔ Certainly not obtained by assuming
- ✔ Are discovered by asking open-ended questions and
- ✔ Listening

The important "what" to this customer was their stated need for reliability in a power generation system for their dairy farm. The "why" was that their cows have to be milked every day, and three days is the maximum storage capacity for raw milk.

When a customer tells you what is important to them, your goal should be to better understand *why* they feel that way.

For investors, the "whys" go beyond demographics and objective measurements to what has greater personal meaning to the client—such as the life goals they are trying to achieve with their investment strategy. It might be caring for a loved one, or other unique personal needs they are trying to satisfy.

Some investment advisors ask mostly closed-ended questions in order to know their customer. They ask customers to select from pre-determined categories that reflect their investment objectives, time horizon, and risk tolerance. Those are similar to questions and suggested strategies employed by so-called robo-advisors. These questions are not likely to get at *why* investors invest. The best advisors know that. Tailoring recommendations based on a dialogue uncovers insights, not merely categorical information, which sets the investment advisor apart from digital tools.

"We care as much about why you are investing
as what you're investing in."

—Edward Jones[19]

Listen

The failure to listen is at the core of many of the problems with presentations and sales efforts in general. Robert Herjavec, one of the stars of the program *Shark Tank,* certainly thinks so. He said he is dismayed by how little some salespeople know or want to know about their customers. In his book, *Think Like a Shark,* he wrote, "We are often impressed (and often surprised) with someone who has anticipated our concerns and is prepared to answer them directly." He added, "Salespeople who start selling without asking questions are like doctors who write prescriptions without asking what ails the patient. In medicine it's called malpractice. In selling it's called stupidity."[20]

Legendary Texas retailer, Jim "Mattress Mack" McIngvale, noted, "Only one in a thousand salespeople listens to what I have to say before launching into their pitch."

Know your customer? Okay, so what's new?

Listening is certainly an essential part of knowing your audience, but knowing your audience isn't a breakthrough idea either. What could be more basic than knowing your customer? What's new—and not so new—is that being *insightfully* knowledgeable is not only pivotal, it is far from obvious, fundamental, or elementary. Understanding an investor's motivations and investment decision criteria is a complex endeavor. You need to have a genuine interest in getting to know your client. It is hard to fake it. You need to ask the right kinds of open-ended questions and listen to the answers through the filter of your life and industry experience.

Know your audience? What's new is the bar of knowing the audience has been raised from being informed to being insightfully knowledgeable. That includes knowledge of the customer, their business, and the key issues the client faces with its constituent groups—their customers, employees, government regulators, and others.

Knowing the audience is not a new idea, but one that is not given adequate priority in presentations.

What's new is that the failure to listen and the negative consequences it creates remain major problems in less-than-effective presentations. Customer interviews using open-ended questions are an essential source of customer knowledge. There are no good substitutes.

"In many cases, an open-ended format can produce vignettes of considerable richness. It is an invaluable tool when you go deeply into particular topics, and is absolutely essential when you are beginning work in an area and need to explore all aspects."

—Norman Bradburn, Seymour Sudman, and Brian Wansink[21]

"You can do five to seven thirty-minute interviews within two business days and learn a ton of information that can completely steer your product in a different direction."

—Jonathan Horowitz, Citrusbyte[22]

There are bonus benefits to listening: Customers like sellers who ask and listen, and likability increases persuasiveness. Questions make conversations more enjoyable. Those who ask and listen are perceived to be more capable. The last point is one made by researchers from Harvard Business School, who found in a study they conducted that people who asked for advice were not perceived to be less capable—but rather smarter and more capable. Assuming and not asking is never a wise strategy. This research makes that point, but also focuses on how asking can eliminate a negative outcome and how doing so can create a positive one that can have an influence on persuasion.[23]

How do you discover insights?

Being good at discovering insights requires learning some of the skills and techniques of a research professional. When research professionals look for insights, they look for what is salient to a customer. Something that is salient stands out and may even be conspicuous. It is something that, based on your judgment and life-experience, seems to be notably important.

Insights differ from information. Table 1 shows four real-world insights from actual sales presentations and how they differ from basic information.

TABLE 1. Insights versus information

Information is the statement of a billionaire's investment objectives as articulated by the CEO and CFO of his company.	An insight: knowing how aggressively he wanted his money managed and why, without the clogged internal filter of his chief lieutenants.
Information is the outline of what a company seeks in a new vendor as contained in the RFP.	An insight: knowing the reason they fired the previous vendor—information that wasn't included in the RFP, but was highly significant to the future of any other seller in attracting and retaining that client.
Information is a statement of the key criteria that a major corporate retirement plan sponsor will use to select an investment manager.	An insight: learning, just before the meeting begins, that there is a major reason the client does not believe in the quality of your product and is not likely to select you for the assignment.
Information is the client's strategy for maintaining brand loyalty, by donating a percentage of sales to charity.	An insight: knowing that the client's customers like that idea and that they prefer a specific charitable organization by a wide margin over others.

In the instances shown, key business insights—not just the basic information about the customers or their stated objectives—were critical to success or failure in winning these accounts. One way to distinguish whether an answer to a question qualifies as an insight or not is to weigh what the client says against your own industry and life experiences. It may take a few follow-up questions to do that. Spontaneous answers to open-ended questions often provide those insights. Spontaneity is important. Let your customers tell you what is on their mind without prompting or fishing for confirmation of your ingoing assumptions. If you are talking to multiple individuals, you want to look for those top-of-mind answers that are consistent across individuals across departments and across locations. When you meet those criteria, you have the basis for making some supportable conclusions about what is generally important to respondents and why. You will know a true insight when you see it.

Open-ended questions prompt responses with a richness not available from checkmarks for categories. The first step in wording these questions is to determine what you want to learn, then compose the question to satisfy it. Look for examples of how others—maybe even those in your own firm—worded similar questions. Use or modify those questions to suit your needs and accomplish your learning objectives.

"One advantage of open-ended questions is that they can uncover uncommon but intelligent opinions on which the (interviewer) would otherwise remain unaware."

—Norman Bradburn, Seymour Sudman, and Brian Wansink.[24]

Questions, learning objectives, and wording questions to satisfy objectives

To understand customer motivations (why the individual and/or institution is investing)…

"What are you most trying to achieve in your life with this investment?"

"What is the investment return meant to enable you to do/ accomplish?"

"Why are you investing this money?"

"When will you begin to use it?"

"What are your key financial priorities and how can we be of help?"

"Can you tell us about the investment products you are using now, or have used before, and your experience and satisfaction with them?"

To solicit your customer's suggestions for what it would take to win the account…

"What would we have to do as your investment manager for you to be highly satisfied with our services?"

"Why is that important to you?"

"What one benefit is most important to you in selecting a provider of these services?"

"What would you suggest that we make sure to do or not do to make our presentation most relevant and helpful to you and your committee?"

"What particular individuals or perspectives—if any—should our presentation be sure to address?"

To uncover something important that might not have been discussed ...

> "Is there anything else you haven't mentioned that you would like us to think about?"

To discover information not provided elsewhere (i.e. When you know the client is replacing an incumbent investment advisor) ...

> "Can you give us a sense of the reasons you're considering replacing your current investment manager/financial advisor?"

To ensure at the start that you're on the right track and clear about the client's objectives ...

> "This is our understanding of your objectives and expectations and our approach to addressing them. Is there anything we missed or that you would like us to be sure to cover?"

If you have a conference call, ask questions in that forum, but still take the opportunity to ask the opening verification question when all of the players are in the room. Confirm whether the consensus that came out of the conference call, which probably was not conducted with the entire committee, is correct. Modify the question this way: "Our review of your RFP and the answers to questions on the conference call told us that these factors are particularly important in your decision. Do we have that right? Is there anything we missed?"

To politely gain some consensus when you have uncovered conflicting opinions about the client's objectives ...

"In talking with some of your employees, they suggested that issues X, Y, and Z were important to them and to the organization. Can you tell us how these issues fit with your priorities in this case?"

When you don't get it or when your initial proposal doesn't fit the client

Be honest about not understanding something about the client's problem and not having a well thought-out solution.

"We just got a much better idea (or still need a better understanding) of what you are looking for than when we came into to the meeting. We would like to step back and give you a revised proposal. We can do that now or as soon as you give us the opportunity to present it."

Assessing answers

Assess the answers to open-ended questions first in terms of what stands out or seems important based on the way the person responds—their tone and conviction. Focus on the most top-of-mind spontaneous answers, though what is said first is not necessarily indicative of what is most important. The first answer might be influenced by the previous question or a comment.

Ask your most important general question first. That way the response won't be tainted by something said before. You can also ask a follow-up question, such as, "Can you think of anything else?" Or, "Is that the only reason for . . . ?"

The order of the respondent's answers may be more a function of the interview situation than a characteristic about what they feel or believe. With open-ended questions, you will obtain a richness of information, with nuance and distinctions. The answers will energize your understanding of the client.

Having said all of this, don't be too quick to seize on the common answers you expect as being indicative of all that is important to your respondent. As Bradburn, Sudman, and Wansink point out,[25] you will be likely to miss more valuable information that would be found by being open to additional answers. It is also true that when you ask longer questions you will get longer answers. Sometimes you need to channel your inner Sherlock Holmes to persist in the insight discovery process.

The biggest drawback of asking open-ended questions is how to classify and tabulate the answers across large numbers of respondents. This is not usually a problem with a limited number of individual clients. Even investment committees are relatively small. The main idea is to ask the right questions and take good notes as you draw conclusions from the answers. You will see patterns emerge or simply find that some answers make more sense than others.

Big problems occur when you don't ask—or you assume that the answers are elsewhere, or in information that you already have.

Finally, what is the setting for the interview? A phone call? Face to face in your office? Your client's office? Regardless, choose the most comfortable place at the most convenient time possible so the interview will be enjoyable, and not awkward.

"Teams that do not include customer interviews in their process whether upfront or strategically in development miss out on a solid foundation for which they base all downstream steps."

—Jonathan Horowitz, Citrusbyte[26]

Personalized investment advice versus digital platforms

Can technology supplant people and their soft/social skills when it comes to understanding the customer? That is one of the issues facing those in the personal advisory channel for financial services. Personalized investment advisors as a group are focused on tailoring their advice to specific life and financial objectives of each particular client. They should be able to provide client-relevant solutions. The advisory channel faces challenges from digital tools and hybrid services, along with the perception of certain market and generational segments that they have the knowledge to make good and suitable investment decisions on their own.

Barron's reported that very few readers had online brokerage relationships in 1995 when they began their digital investor column—

largely because there were few such options. Barron's cites a 2017 Merrill Lynch survey which found that 40 percent of Americans are using online or mobile portals to manage some aspects of their investments. According to Barron's another Merrill Lynch survey of their wealth management clients showed that 13 percent of respondents are using a robo-advisor, but that level of usage increases to 22 percent for millennials.[27]

In a separate study, Merrill Lynch found that affluent millennials value the advice of a financial advisor, but expect that advice to include proof of effectiveness and to be adapted to the client's specific needs and not be based on an arbitrary business model. [28]

Despite the growing use of online options, most individual investors count on the personal relationship with a financial advisor as their primary source for financial guidance. A recent Wells Fargo/Gallup poll showed that over 47 percent of investors prefer a strong relationship with a personal financial advisor for financial advice versus 23 percent who prefer digital tools. Among investors, eighteen to forty-nine, the preference for a personal financial advisor declined, but remained the top choice. [29]

One such digital tool, Financial Engines, a strictly Internet-based investment advisory service when inaugurated twenty years ago, is now a hybrid model that offers personal investment guidance in 123 offices nationwide, competing with those in the full-service advisory channel. It seems there is a slow creep toward the realization that personal attention is still needed and valued. Conventional wisdom is that millennials and most investors under fifty years of age are more knowledgeable and self-sufficient about investments than previous generations. As such, they should be less inclined to use an advisory channel. Financial Engines is bucking that generational assumption with a renewed focus on personal attention. The use of hybrid and digital investment tools is significant and probably growing. Full service advisors are adding their own digital platforms.

Everyone in financial services has observed and/or experienced the recent major shift toward passive investments such as index funds and ETFs (exchange-traded funds) and away from active management.

Both streams take money away from the people who would manage or help manage it.

The question to be determined is whether the pendulum will swing back to the advisory channel and active management, especially in bear markets. As one noted West Coast asset manager put it, what investors in index funds are guaranteed is matching the gains of the index. They are also guaranteed to absorb identical losses.

Though some individual investors have moved away from the advisory channel, personalized investment advisory services are alive and (reasonably) well. This is also true in the world of institutional investments. The challenge for those in the individual advisory channel is to become even better at knowing and understanding individual clients and their objectives. That's the reason clients choose them over self-directed or digital options in the first place.

Engagement rings and engaged investors

If you buy anything at Borsheims, the Berkshire-Hathaway-owned, fine jewelry store in Omaha, Nebraska, you will see a quote from Warren Buffett on your receipt: "If you don't know jewelry, know your jeweler." One could easily change the quote to read: "If you don't know your investments, know your investment advisor."

Many affluent and emerging affluent clients don't know and don't care to know the details about investing. But they do know when an advisor makes a sincere effort to get to know them and recommends investment products and solutions that are tailored to suit their needs.

When virtually any prospective client sees that a seller in an advisory role is working to perfect their understanding in order to select the right product at the right price from the display case, they are more likely to become a customer. This is the formula that made Borsheims one of the largest independent jewelry stores in the nation, and one that sets many investment advisors apart from their competitors.

The issue for many financial and investment advisors is to determine what the main source is of their added value versus digital tools. Is it the investment performance they offer, their ability to better understand their clients in order to steer them to investments that best suit their goals, or some of both?

Many investment advisors have a fixed set of asset allocation portfolios ranging from conservative to moderate-conservative, to moderate-aggressive, to aggressive. Let's say that the performance of these portfolios is comparable to those offered by robo or hybrid services. If that is the case, it has to be the superior ability to obtain the client insights needed to ensure the right client-portfolio choice, and the confidence the advisor inspires in the customer that the investment option recommended is the one best suited to them.

A cursory, boilerplate questionnaire is not likely to accomplish that goal. Most any customer will notice the difference in the effort to understand them and their goals first before making a recommendation that is meant to satisfy them. That usually means making a superior effort to listen. A personal investment advisor, or any registered representative, should be better at discovering investor insights and acting on them than a robot.

The best financial advisors ask open-ended questions in a conversational format. That enables them to learn about distinctions across categories in ways that digital services cannot. The ability to personally interview customers is the proven, meaningful differential advantage to be leveraged, not squandered.

As a presenter, you want a deep and accurate understanding of the customer before you enter the meeting room. You want a proposal that is based on that foundation and is the result of a logical process beginning with that premise. You want to lay out that logic to the customer upfront. If the customer accepts the premise, and you follow the rules of logic, they should accept your conclusion and may even be two steps ahead of you in getting there.

The presenter wants that initial proposal to fit the client as well as possible from the outset—knowing it won't be a perfect fit at that point and will need alterations, but that any alterations will likely be minor. The goal is a perfect fit and a highly satisfied customer.

Custom tailoring was a big part of how I achieved my most successful presentations in advertising and investment management.

They were built from the ground up based on customer insights. All our capabilities were tied to how they helped the client. The focus was always on the client and creating the best fit with their needs.

Did have I have all of the insights I needed to do that? No. I used whatever insights I had about the customer to be more tailored than off the rack and then used client feedback to make the modifications needed to create a winning customer fit.

Takeaways: How to discover insights

- Have a genuine interest. Customers will see a token effort as just that.
- Ask the right kinds of open-ended questions.
- Follow up because the first answers may not be the only or the most important ones.
- Ask verification questions when all of the players are in the room.
- Have a survey or research professional's mindset whenever you interview anyone—try to make the interview enjoyable, not awkward or boring.
- Set your learning objectives before you word your questions.
- Listen and assess the answers for what, based on your life and industry experience, is notable, stands out, or seems to be at the heart of the matter.
- Always be vigilant, ready to ask to clarify and verify.
- Remember that a single question can be a game changer.

CHAPTER 4

Don't Pull Your Presentation Off the Rack

A custom-tailored presentation fits any particular customer better than a standard presentation that boasts about what is generically good about your product or service. Regardless of the strength of your story, you will be more persuasive when you tailor it to what is most meaningful to your client. Relevance is somewhat about respect, asking questions, and listening carefully to the answers. Failing to be more respectful and relevant to the client is a major reason firms with superior credentials don't always win. Being relevantly connected tells your client that you appreciate their business. You humbly but confidently believe—based on the relevant evidence that you've provided—that you merit the win.

Look at your presentations the way a good tailor looks at an altered garment, meticulously reviewing every detail, ensuring that everything about it fits the customer precisely. Clearly, if you want every aspect of your presentation to address your client's needs and connect to their matter at hand, a standard, off-the-rack presentation will not meet the goal. Even worse, a one-size-fits-all presentation can derail a potential sale, lessen your credibility, and even damage your long-term reputation.

The saga of one prominent company's attempt to sign a reigning NBA superstar to a lucrative sneaker contract provides a chamber-of-horrors example. The player was Stephen Curry and the bidders were Nike and Under Armour. In the end, Curry left Nike for Under Armour. As a result, Under Armour gained a major foothold in the high-end sneaker business, and Nike ultimately lost a similar order of magnitude in what was, at the time, an almost 90 percent share of that market.

You may have heard this story. The first lesson it provides is about what can happen to anyone who creates PowerPoint presentations in which the only alteration made from one prospective client to another is changing the customer's name on the cover page.

According to the accounts from ESPN,[30] the presentation to Stephen Curry and his father at Nike's headquarters got off to a bad start. A person from Nike mispronounced Curry's first name, calling him Steph-*on* instead of Stephen. Next it became painfully obvious that the presentation was pulled off the shelf, and not specifically tailored to Curry when one slide still contained the name of another NBA player from a previous presentation.

The clear conclusion of this maybe not-uncommon example is: if all you do to customize your presentation is put the client's name on the cover, you've missed the point and lost an opportunity to be optimally persuasive.

Earlier, Curry had made it clear that he was very interested in running his own Nike basketball camp. That offer was totally muddled.

Curry and his father left the meeting perplexed at the seeming lack of respect for them and their needs. It was clear to Curry's father that Nike was not intending to make his son a "signature athlete." This resurfaced the disappointment Curry experienced by being underestimated for his entire career up to the point of being named the NBA's Most Valuable Player. This was another insight that was lost in the Nike pitch.

Whether it was due to Nike's failure to read the tea leaves or simply the mistake of taking a client for granted, Under Armour was able to step into the breach. Their courtship of Curry had begun a year earlier. Curry had been impressed with how Under Armour treated a rookie on his team—sending boxes of gear that only superstars received. If Under Armour treated a rookie that way, they would surely treat Curry in a manner he deserved.

What client does not want to feel important to their financial advisor? Clients who know their assets are modest, in comparison to other clients, appreciate an advisor who shows they care and value their business.

Many different issues were part of the inherent failure of a canned presentation like this one. Most prominent among them is the lack of insightful knowledge and/or the failure to act on that knowledge. Obviously, little effort was made to carefully tailor the presentation to Curry's known motivations and preferences.

This story shows how and why the seller with the best credentials, capabilities, and reputation doesn't always win. Conversely it indicates that any seller with a competitive product can gain an edge with a more genuine customer focus and a commitment to show how what they provide best fulfills that particular customer's specific goals.

Do prominent firms agree that they need to do more than go through the motions of convincing prospective clients that they value their business? Not all of them.

A principal in one the nation's most prominent institutional asset managers once told me that their salespeople were almost superfluous. Their investment performance, investment discipline, people, and their client roster were as impressive as it gets. In his opinion, their services almost sold themselves. But even that organization was vulnerable to a competitor that made a better effort to understand the client and tailored their message and offering accordingly.

On several occasions I won out over more credentialed competitors with greater social proof than my firm had for its products. I attribute that success to trying harder than they did to get to the heart of the matter for the client, and adjusting everything in my presentations to show that my firm could best satisfy those particularly important needs.

Most clients don't want their unique interests taken for granted. Taking a highly client-relevant approach is important for every seller because it's important to most every buyer.

The failure of a path-breaking company to attract an investor

The same pitfalls that torpedoed Nike's pitch can afflict sophisticated, high-stakes investment presentations too. Even leading-edge organizations can fall victim to taking customers for granted by being more consumed with telling their story than ensuring that it relates to what the customer needs and wants to hear.

This story is an example of how you can lose an investor even when you have many of the key ingredients to be successfully persuasive. The seller was the founder and CEO of a company that had social proof, urgency, disruptive technology, great consumer appeal, and dramatic growth.

This individual started a path-breaking personal-services company with uniquely beneficial technology and deserved enormous credit for what he accomplished. Yet he may have taken one investor's interest a bit too much for granted and, with that attitude, failed to inspire the confidence the investor needed to get on board. This was an example of believing in the appeal of your story, without doing the work to understand what your customer needs and wants to know to be convinced that you merit their investment.

When that founder of a worldwide enterprise that had revolutionized personal, urban transportation came to a major investment manager seeking additional funding, the investment manager and its portfolio managers and analysts had seen the pitch book before the founder arrived. They knew that the founder's company's app-based service had been quickly adopted by urban dwellers in dozens of countries and over two hundred cities.

That service featured mobile computer technology that transformed the way people move within cities to shop, have dinner, go to the office, visit friends, and comfortably and safely get home afterward. You may have used this service and, if you have, you are probably among the millions of highly satisfied customers.

The company's story was truly impressive. It had excellent prospects for continued dramatic growth. Few qualified institutional investors didn't give this opportunity a serious look and participate in the latest round of funding. In fact, many other major investment managers had already chosen to invest. The company had the added credibility that an impressive roster of investors provides. This gave the company what Robert Cialdini, the acclaimed author on the subject of influence, calls social proof, based on that concept from psychology.[31]

Social proof—or simply referenceable clients—is a powerful contributor to what makes someone persuasive. That does not mean it is a legitimate gauge of the worth of a product—whether that product is an investment opportunity or something else. The Madoff Ponzi scheme in New York gained many investors who were later burned, in part, because they were impressed with Madoff's impressive list of clients along with impressive returns (that turned out to be fraudulent). Despite the glaring exceptions, social proof is still generally a valid positive indicator of the seller's ability to have satisfied customers.

The personal transportation company had a list of prominent investors ranging from a Wall Street investment bank to Hollywood stars. However, after listening to the founder's pitch, this particular asset management firm declined to get on board. Why? Because the decision-makers there felt that he was a bit too overconfident given the challenges his company faced. His attitude created concern about his judgment and how steadfast he would be in furthering the interests of his investors. In their view, this overconfident streak would likely creep into and shape how he made future business decisions. The firm simply lacked sufficient conviction in the founder to invest in his company.

Was this also a case of not liking and trusting the founder? Or was it a result of not liking or trusting the founder because of the way he'd conducted himself during the presentation? Maybe it was a bit of both.

What is controllable about likability? Other than being a likable person to begin with, what can a seller do to satisfy that criterion? Listen.

Listening is something that any presenter can do to be more well liked—or at least be less disliked. Customers like sellers who ask and listen but don't assume.

Customers want sellers who are responsive to their concerns. The failure to listen and to want to hear what clients have to say is almost always a bad start for any seller who depends on a high level of client confidence to succeed.

The anatomy of a presentation failure

In hindsight, the decision by this particular investment manager to decline to invest likely turned out to be a mistake—in the short run, at least. The valuation estimates of the company soared. Even so, that didn't change the way the investment firm or its management team viewed its decision.

What happened in that meeting room killed the founder's funding request. The problem wasn't what was in the pitch book, or the story about the company's merits, or the investment opportunity itself. It was, to large degree, the founder's failure to adequately meet the special evaluative criteria this particular investment manager employed for the kind of investment that was being requested.

So what are the implications for being more successfully persuasive?

The investment opportunity in question was a "story stock," a stock in which an investment manager bets on the promise of future growth. At this point, there are no substantial assets or even profitable income streams on which to base or justify valuations. There are no forests or oil reserves on the balance sheet. The decision is heavily predicated on the investment manager's confidence in the company's management team. If the management team doesn't sufficiently address the multiple perspectives in the room—and inspire confidence in those individuals while doing so—the investment manager is not going to commit.

So what more concrete steps should be taken? How can these types of presentations be more effective? When I helped launch a new hedge fund, my focus was on helping the portfolio manager of that fund relate to our potential investors and instill confidence that their investment in him was justified. His "story" product had a limited track record with the new investment strategy he proposed, even though he had a long and distinguished record with an international stock fund focused on the same region of the world. But the personal fit between this fund manager and his potential investors was the key criterion to successfully persuade clients to invest. The case to be made was more about *him* than it was about historical returns he'd generated in related products. Any potential sale was based on the buyer's confidence in the portfolio manager.

One of the first things to do in making such a pitch is to explain the client's perspective. That would be to caution a presenter that the client's decision is based as much or more on their confidence in the founder or individual portfolio manager as on the merits of the investment opportunity itself. The main reason for losing a pitch like that would be the lack of rapport they develop with the client and the inability to instill confidence. The presenter needs to inject a degree of humility into the presentation. Asking a client to invest in something based on future earnings and little in the way of assets to support the company's current valuation is not easy. Presenters who don't express a degree of humility in the face of that challenge are likely to come across as overly confident. That could be an impression that kills the deal.

The presenter has to be aware of those motivations and address them with their demeanor and their justification for being able to fulfill the objectives they create.

Knowing your client means asking questions and listening to the answers. Verify that what you intend to present is on the right track with the client's expectations and ensure that you cover what they most want you to cover. At least ask before launching into your pitch.

There is a link between listening and confidence. If a founder or CEO does not seem to care to listen to his potential investors, what does that say about how much that person cares about meeting the investor expectations they create? Understanding that potential link and ensuring that you address what your client wants to address is another soft and potentially pivotal skill.

The founder of the personal transportation service may have assumed he had a story strong enough to carry the day. It had clearly worked with other investors prior to the meeting with this one. But he didn't seem to fully appreciate the key concerns and varying perspectives in the audience for that next investor. He may have wrongly assumed that the approach he used before would work again and may have never thought of the need to tailor it to better fit that investor. In this case, with this investor, he failed to get the nod.

A different path could have been taken. There is a more tailored and customer-aware fork in every presentation road.

CHAPTER 5

Take the Bespoke Fork in the Presentation Road

I f your job is in marketing or sales, you are charged with sourcing and acquiring customers for your organization's products and services. You know the distinctive features and advantages of those products and services. You have been trained to have that product knowledge. Additionally, your organization holds a particular view about how it should be portrayed when communicating with current and prospective customers. You must explain your corporate mission and adhere to it. Your organization's brand identity stems from what you say and do.

What you can't obtain via internal resources and training alone, however, is the knowledge of what a specific customer seeks in a sales encounter. Your company helps you know the product. Understanding the customer is up to you.

You have a choice between two paths: lay out your best case for your product and let your customer decide whether it's right for them, or start with a blank slate for each customer and address their unique needs. In the first approach, you make an enthusiastic pitch about what your products do and why they do it better than others. Key attributes are highlighted in isolation apart from the known customer-specific needs they address.

You can make your pitch a masterpiece, extolling your product's superior features versus the competition. You can lay out all of the most significant differential advantages right there on the table. You are counting on your customers to select the features that resonate with them, and that you have enough of those relevant attributes to lead the customer to select you. If you represent a leading organization with some of the best products in the industry, you may feel particularly self-assured about what you have to say and its objective customer appeal. A confident presenter with a strong product can win and close the sale, but this doesn't mean you'll be optimally effective over repeated trials.

In contrast, you could paint the picture differently. You could start with that blank canvas about your customer, rather than with preconceived ideas or preset presentation content. You listen to each buyer, carefully assessing their motivations and what they need to hear from you to make a decision, and then craft your presentation accordingly. This is the "bespoke" approach. Bespoke is a generic term meaning custom-made. But it has a much richer meaning in Britain.

"Each customer is a fresh and unique canvas to us."

—Henry Poole, British bespoke tailor

In Britain, bespoke means handmade and designed to fit the client perfectly. The term originated over two hundred years ago. When a customer selected cloth for a garment, it was said to "be spoken for." Those three words were quaintly contracted to *bespoke*. If you see an offer to go to a local hotel to be fitted for a "bespoke suit" by a traveling group of tailors, be wary. It doesn't mean what it means in Britain. If you see an offer for a bespoke garment made almost anywhere else, it won't be truly bespoke.

According to the British Bespoke Tailors Association, which is very protective of the bespoke tradition, to be considered truly *bespoke*, a garment must be handmade from scratch to fit the exact measurements of the client. If you want to purchase a bespoke suit from these quintessentially customer-focused tailors, you won't find them online or anywhere except Savile Row in London.

The services of a true bespoke tailor involve much more than taking physical measurements and manufacturing an item of clothing. They are marked by a commitment to listen to client feedback and make the necessary alterations to produce a garment that both fits the client physically *and* suits the client's lifestyle across a spectrum of life experiences.

Many elements of a bespoke approach make it a useful way for sellers to think about how to create investment presentations, and many other presentations, that successfully fit their clients and make the sale. One element is that British Bespoke tailors are among the most client-relevant businesses in the world. Client relevance is the crucial element in persuasive communications.

The *Oxford American Dictionary* defines relevance as "closely connected or appropriate to the matter at hand." I would define a successfully persuasive presentation for investment management, and most any other business, as one that closely connects every aspect of the story to how and why it satisfies the particular client's unique *matter at hand*. Bespoke is an apt metaphor for what it takes to accomplish this goal.

First, bespoke is all about the client. The bespoke process begins not with exact physical measurements. That is step two. Step one starts with a conversation between the tailor and the client. The purpose is to better understand the work and non-work lives of the client, and the various settings in which the garment will be worn. The Private Tailors at Gieves and Hawkes, a British Bespoke Tailor that has served princes, kings, and soccer stars for more than 150 years, say that different customers wear the same suit for different purposes in different environments. That information would qualify as an insight for me. That underlying point is succinctly reinforced by lecturers at MIT's Sloan School of Management. "The reasons customers buy the exact same product," they say, "vary from account to account."[32] One-size-fits-all doesn't work on Savile Row or in broader marketing contexts either.

The flagship mutual fund we discussed in detail earlier, the Black-Rock Global Allocation Fund, provided a vintage example of this point. Like all mutual funds, it was managed in the exact same way for each shareholder, as per the prospectus. Yet investor motivations for investing in that fund varied greatly from shareholder to shareholder. Some wanted total return. Some wanted global exposure. Others wanted a foundation fund with excellent risk versus return characteristics that other, more narrowly defined funds could be built around.

In many cases, the script has to change, because the client wants you to change it. This happens with customers across industries. This point could not be more succinctly made than by this comment from a friend and long-time, medical director for Merck, Golden Zenon III, who said, "Some doctors want to talk extensively about the data for the efficacy of the drug, others want the Cliff Notes, and some want to discuss how it can save the world." Even with all of the data on individual physicians and their prescription histories, understanding these preferences requires taking the extra steps of asking, listening to, and getting to know these doctors' preferences over time.

Bespoke tailors interview their clients to learn about their tastes and lifestyle. They do that, in part, because they don't want to assume common motivations. They know that even in the somewhat narrow segment of the population that is their target audience there are wide variations from client to client.

The interviews conducted by the private tailor are designed to uncover such details in order to paint a complete picture of the client, and lay the foundation for a long-term relationship based on trust. The questions a private tailor asks a customer can seem trivial. One could be whether a client carries a slim wallet or one chock full of credit cards, currency, and checks. The size of the wallet will affect the cut of the suit.

Just as a bespoke tailor needs more than physical measurements to best suit their client's needs, a financial services firm needs to know about why their clients are investing and their life goals, not just boilerplate information such as age, income, asset levels, risk tolerance, and basic investment objectives such as growth or income. If the client is an institution, a financial services firm needs to know that organization's profile, and the perspectives, motivations, and fears of key decision-makers. These insights are the foundation for all steps that follow.

Financial services firms want to get to know their clients and forge long-term client relationships. Those insights can't be discovered without asking the right kinds of questions and listening to the answers.

The second goal of the tailor's initial client conversations is to create a prototype for the custom-made garment that will eventually fit the client in all the relevant dimensions. In investment management, the financial advisor wants to create and deliver an initial investment proposal—perhaps a sample portfolio—that is as well-suited to the client as it can be for that first, and maybe only, meeting before the client makes a decision.

Another reason bespoke is an apt metaphor is that the initial recommendation—in this case the first iteration of the garment—almost always needs alterations. Despite careful preparation and due diligence, investment (and other) proposals don't fit the client perfectly and also require alterations. The ability to adapt is an important attribute for a bespoke tailor as well as an investment management salesperson.

Gieves and Hawkes, founded in 1771, and located at No. 1 Savile Row, is one of London's oldest and most famous bespoke tailors, counting among its clients: Winston Churchill, David Beckham, and Prince Charles, and Prince William. It is a great example of a company that knows the importance of adapting to suit its clients' objectives and changing life circumstances.

After the cutter at Gieves and Hawkes crafts the first iteration of a garment, it may take several fittings and sets of alterations to achieve the desired fit, each iteration becoming ever more personalized and precise. As needed, the client returns for additional fittings. After the final fitting, the tailor makes "any further adjustments as required to ensure that the garment does not leave the store until it's an absolutely perfect fit."[33] Certainly, that seems like a worthy aspirational goal for any investment sales effort. The inability to make necessary alterations is one major reason sales efforts fall short.

The bespoke tailor's customer is buying the expectation that they will look and feel better in a handmade garment than one taken off the rack. Investment managers are selling the expectations of future performance, a variable outcome that cannot be guaranteed. The charge for the investment manager or financial advisor is to instill confidence that their clients' assets will be managed to satisfy mutually agreed-upon, realistic expectations and provide those clients with evidence that their confidence is justified.

Amid all these considerations, bespoke tailors are also concerned about how clients relate to their own audiences. That audience could be their customers, employees, managers, social contacts, or members of the customer's family.

Mutual fund companies who administer 401(k) plans need to know and work with the corporate plan sponsor. They need to assist those plan sponsors in the design of the investment menu and help employees make the best use of those investments in order to meet their retirement and other goals. These companies also have to support the business-building efforts of the financial advisors who sell their products to the ultimate investor.

The bespoke interview experience

The bespoke tailoring process begins with a conversation between the tailor and the client. For that initial conversation, the customer arrives at the shop and is greeted by the private tailor and ushered into a well-appointed room with comfortable chairs. Tea and coffee and biscuits are served with real china. This is British hospitality in its simplest, most civilized form. The setting should be appropriate for a customer who is there to buy a single custom-made garment at a cost of $10,000 to $15,000, or even more. As they say in Britain, truly bespoke suits are not merely clothes; they are "investment pieces."

The tailor uses what is learned in that first conversation to start to form a picture of the customer and their unique requirements. The tailor next gently steers the customer toward basic designs, including cloth and cut, which seem to match their picture of the customer. The tailor then verifies that this initial pattern meets with the customer's approval. If so, it becomes the pattern from which the eventual garment will be created. Above all, the tailor wants to ensure there is complete harmony of design and customer objective. Only then are the exact physical measurements taken. Ultimately, a handmade garment will be crafted to those specifications.

Don't have a conversation with a 5-star client in a 2-star conference room.

I don't remember ever being in a meeting in England where I wasn't offered tea or coffee—and biscuits—with porcelain, not paper cups. In fact, I was always struck by the contrast between those encounters and many of the client meetings in our offices. Many meeting rooms I used for client meetings were in need of a major makeover.

This was never more apparent than when the managing director and part owner of the highest-rated luxury hotel group in Hong Kong came to our offices in Princeton. He had retained Morgan Stanley—the ultimate white-shoe Wall Street firm—to introduce him to variety of asset managers in the United States.

We were given very short notice to set up the meeting. I found the best available meeting room. It had no windows, a laminated conference table, and stark walls with generic, corporate-issue artwork, and Steelcase chairs. We had Styrofoam cups for coffee and soda. No porcelain.

Our prospective client arrived—impeccably dressed in his custom-tailored suit, perhaps made by a bespoke tailor in London or a fine custom tailor in Hong Kong. This man was a protégé of the wealthiest person in Hong Kong—one of the richest people in the world. He customarily hosted the elite from that city and around the globe at his hotels. Few people on the planet knew more about what it meant to have the absolute highest level of guest services than this man. Because I'd stayed at his hotels—on company business—I knew this firsthand.

But here I was, trapped in a physical space that couldn't possibly meet his standards. I knew we didn't look and feel like the kind of firm he wanted to entrust with his considerable assets.

I don't think even the best investment performance would have convinced him to select us. It felt like that much of a mismatch.

In the end, he didn't place any of his portfolio assets with us. We didn't fit what he was looking for—and that was true on multiple fronts—but most important perhaps, our pitch and our team never quite recovered from his negative first impressions.

I needed one of the rooms on what some called the "opulent" executive floors at our headquarters in the World Financial Center in New York. Even now, I believe—in this case—choosing that setting *alone* would have dramatically increased our chances of being selected by this particular client. He would have appreciated the environment, the attention to detail, and the importance we placed on his visit.

Isn't the customer of a bespoke tailor and what they want in a custom-tailored product a lot like your investment client? Isn't this an appropriate model for that initial conversation? Isn't that the way your client would like to be treated?

Most individual and institutional investors place their assets (of much greater consequence than an investment in a bespoke garment) with advisors. It follows that these investors should merit at least the quality of conversation and physical setting for that relationship that a British bespoke tailor provides.

The initial presentation to any client is like a first fitting.

The stories discussed so far are all about adapting to improve the product-customer fit. Many of the presentations described failed or almost failed before they succeeded. Virtually none of them proceeded unimpeded from the start to a successful conclusion.

Initial meetings or new business presentations are first fittings to determine how well the presenter and the presenter's proposal suit the client. The fitting part is embedded in the dialogue between the buyer and the seller.

Though many of the presentations described initially went wrong, the negatives that were discovered had a silver lining. They pointed out the steps needed to alter those presentations to better fit with the client. This is the prize to focus on. The better the customer feedback you have, the better able you are able to continuously make the necessary alterations that will produce the desired outcome. That iterative process is the essence of a bespoke approach.

A bespoke approach fits with an emerging—or restored sales paradigm.

The bespoke metaphor may also be a particularly timely one for meeting what B2B customers want from sellers—the trusted advisor benefit. Let's call it a trusted tailor to extend the metaphor. In either case, the intended customer benefits are the same.

According to a 2016 Gallup study, B2B buyers want more than discussions about product and price—they want sellers who help their customers' businesses grow. "This approach," say the authors of the study, "requires a differentiated sales strategy—one that is advisory, tailored to each customer, and provides valuable insights."[34]

This is what buyers said they need, want, and expect from sellers. It is what buyers said they are not getting from sellers. It is why Gallup found that that over 71 percent of those surveyed said that they are considering taking their business elsewhere. While the importance of these factors may be heightened by challenging business and economic environments, buyers have largely always wanted to do business with sellers who best provided those benefits.

This may not be news to those who believe they have had this kind of commitment and provided these kinds of benefits to their clients all along. But that commitment has to be executed. That does not appear to be the case for buyers who say they are ready to walk away from current relationships.

The implications from the Gallup study provide strong empirical support for the validity and value of a tailored approach. The study suggests the need for a sales paradigm that positions sellers to find solutions that are not taken off-the-rack but rather precisely well-suited to their clients and their specific business needs. A bespoke approach can do all of these things and more.

How tailored are your presentations to your customer?

Is the guiding principle for your presentations to demonstrate the best fit between what you do and what your customers are looking for and how your product's key attributes address the client's matter at hand? Or is your presentation heavily based on organizational credentials and accomplishments?

Are your presentations effective in demonstrating the strengths of your product? If they excel on that dimension, are they equally effective in talking about how those strengths fit the unique needs of a specific customer? If the answer is yes, you are already tailoring your presentations in ways that will help make you more persuasive. If the answer is no, there are reasons for you to go back and talk to your customers and shift the focus back to them.

Did I reach an ideal level of tailoring in all aspects of all of my presentations? No. Did the successful ones each tailor the proposal to key, known customer insights? Yes, absolutely.

Create the relevant links that are at the core of great persuasion.

When you know your audience well enough to tailor your presentation to their motivations and objectives, you will be more believable, persuasive, and ultimately successful. There is support for the validity of this view from theory and research in behavioral economics and psychology. In a discussion about how to write a persuasive message, Daniel Kahneman, winner of the Nobel Prize in economics, poses this question and answers it in the following way: "How do you know that a statement is true? If it is strongly linked by logic or association to other beliefs or preferences you hold, or it comes from a source you trust and like . . ."[35]

What does this mean for making statements about your organization in persuasive presentation materials? Let's say that you have this known insight about your customer—that they have not been happy with the manager turnover at their current investment advisor. They will choose the firm that shows it can keep the people their clients count on. You have two approaches you could take in your presentation to this customer

Approach A

You could rely on this point in your "About Us" page to speak for itself: "Our managers have an average of twenty years with the firm and eighteen years of investment experience."

Or

Approach B

You could say this to that same customer: "At Asset Manager 'T' we make a top-down commitment and expend a great deal of effort to maintain stability in our organization and consistency in our investment process. Because of that, our managers have an average of twenty years with the firm and eighteen years of investment experience. That is why we can satisfy your concerns about manager turnover and have a person that you can count on to be here and do what they say they will do now and in the future."

Approach A is simply to lay out that credential and let the customer determine if it resonates with them. Approach B takes that otherwise isolated attribute, expands on it, and puts it in the context of solving the customer's problem. This is not a subtle distinction. Evidence laid out in a smorgasbord fashion will not have as much impact as telling the client what is really good on the menu, given their tastes and preferences. That's guidance. That's marketing. That's selling.

I was a more confident and effective presenter when I had relevant knowledge. From my time in advertising through my career in investment management, I always thought that talking about credentials and accomplishments in isolation of how they helped the customer was what one my colleagues at Y&R called "jumping on the capabilities bandwagon."

What I did and learned at Y&R had a great deal to do with how I created investment management and sales presentations at Merrill Lynch. For instance, whenever the agency was asked to do a capabilities presentation for a client, the titles on the presentation boards said "Relevant Capabilities," not "Capabilities." This was a purposeful decision, backed up by what we said. We didn't just show the reel of our top commercials. We talked about our key successes with products in industries similar to those of the prospective client. If our best commercials were relevant to the client, we included them; if not, we excluded them. In short, we made the decision to avoid touting attributes and achievements with limited meaning to our clients and their customers. We also encouraged our clients not do that in their own marketing communications.

When I began new business presentations at Merrill Lynch, I talked about our credentials as an investment management firm and explained what was in it for the client. Many financial services and professional services presentations and promotional statements on websites still talk about company superlatives without explicitly matching them to customer needs. That may be so because they are successful, highly capable companies, eager to jump on the capabilities bandwagon, spread that good news, and hopefully impress their clients by doing so.

"Speak at great length about the history of your organization and its glorious achievements."

—Chris Anderson, head of TED, on how to ruin a presentation.[36]

Pages in many presentations have titles like "Our Resources" and "About Us." These are lists of credentials and achievements, but typically they are much more about the seller than how those qualities help any customer. If you use pages like these, program greater relevance into them by modifying the titles to read "Relevant Resources" and "About Us and How We Can Help."

You might say, with good reason, that your company is what it is, and that you are not going to change that from client to client. By taking a bespoke approach, you are not deviating from your company mission, corporate principles, or personality. You are demonstrating how what you do and how you do it addresses your client's distinct preferences and motivations. But what you should not do is make a statement of who you are that fails to explain how that creates satisfied clients. Draw those links yourself. Don't rely on your customer to make those deductions even though they may do so.

If you know that manager turnover was an issue for a prospective client, talk at some length about your organization's management continuity and how you achieved it. If the issue was lack of ongoing communications in person or otherwise, provide your assurances or evidence that you would do better. Strike a balance between the worthy goal of telling customers what is good about your organization and telling them how your key attributes directly address the benefits they seek. Give the most weight to the client connection.

The off-the-rack to bespoke continuum

Virtually any presentation can be positioned along a continuum between off-the-rack and bespoke. The success of a presentation often can be determined by:

- the extent to which it is canned versus customized.
- whether it makes relevant connections to the audience or not.
- whether it is based on specific, known customer insights or on assumed information.

TABLE 2. Differing approaches

Off-the-rack	Bespoke
Generalized audience knowledge	Insightful knowledge
Inventories of capabilities	Relevantly connected capabilities
Implicit connections to the audience	Explicitly meaningful connections
Belief in the product	Belief in how product helps the customer
What is generically good about your product	What about the product is good for the specific customer
Blind faith in the product fit	Evidence for confidence in the fit
What you want to say	What the customer wants and needs to hear

The key difference between canned and customized presentations is often a matter of emphasis. By objectively thinking about where your presentations fit along the continuum, you can assess how well you balance knowing and believing in your product versus truly understanding how well your product's key features and advantages benefit your client.

Look at a few of your client presentations and see where you would place each along the continuum between off the rack and bespoke.

- Does it effectively portray what your organization does?
- Is it equally effective at explicitly connecting key attributes to what your customer wants and needs?
- Is the guiding principle for your presentations to demonstrate the best fit between what you do and what your customers are looking for, or on the superiority of your product?
- Is your presentation heavily based on organizational credentials and accomplishments, or how your product's key attributes address the client's matter at hand?
- Are you more comfortable and confident when you have useful, advance knowledge about what your customer is looking for, and less confident and comfortable when you lack that information?

In a standard presentation, you still have to know and believe in your product. A bespoke presentation takes that one step further. When you have more insightful knowledge about your audience, you have the foundation for believing how your product fits the needs of that particular customer, enhancing your confidence and persuasiveness. You're not *assuming* that you have that fit; you have solid evidence for it. In turn, your confidence in that fit inspires confidence on the part of your audience.

Why canned presentations are less effective.

Canned presentations lack relevant connections. The reason for this is simple: one-size-fits-all presentations fail to recognize that each specific audience/prospect has its own unique, highly specific needs. There is no relevant connection if the product attributes touted are not directly linked to the customer's specific wants and needs.

If your presentation doesn't vary from prospective client to prospective client—other than the name on the cover page and a basic articulation of that client's objectives gleaned from the RFP or the client's website—you haven't really tailored anything to them at all. You've clearly missed a chance to draw meaningful, logical links between your organization and your customer. If you don't know anything more about your audience than the basic reason it seeks your help, you've probably already lost out to a competitor who has deeper, more meaningful, and actionable information.

Don't send a broadcast message to a narrowly defined audience.

Advertising is transmitting the same message to a targeted, but still broad audience. Personal persuasive communications are about delivering a tailored message to an extremely narrowly defined audience— maybe even an audience of one. No presenter should want to send a broadcast, undifferentiated message to a small group of recipients with unique needs, motivations, beliefs, and preferences. If you lack insightful knowledge about your customer, there is the tendency to fall back on what you know about yourself and your organization, rather than how you solve the customer's problem. Secretly, you hope you have enough firepower to carry the day. A presenter doesn't need to know any information about the customer to talk about what their company does. That can be done in a vacuum.

The top companies with the best products don't always win.

Presenters who have the most formidable organizational strengths and objective product advantages are often the same ones who lean most heavily on generic strengths and attributes, rather than taking the crucial next step to demonstrate how and why those features specifically address the customer's matter at hand. Many of the most established firms with the most impressive client rosters are hard to beat—but they don't win every time.

There are many things that presenters with at least relatively comparable capabilities can do to prevail. Using a bespoke perspective and approach is one of those ways. Customers know and appreciate when the seller makes a concerted effort to better understand their particular matter at hand. For many of those buyers—who may feel misunderstood, underappreciated, or even ignored—they are often entirely willing to forego ostensibly superior product benefits and take their business elsewhere to find a seller who carefully listens and tailors the proposed solution to specifically suit their needs.

CHAPTER 6

Benchmark Against Best Practices

As I was first thinking about this book, I wanted to look at state-of-the-art business presentations from prominent and successful companies to see how they balanced talking about themselves with how they benefited their customers. I wanted to see where they fit on the standard to customized presentation spectrum. Senior executives from these companies gave me examples of actual, current, and complete proprietary presentations. I did a content analysis of each. One of the presentations was from a major multinational asset manager, another from a multinational management consulting firm.

The more specific purpose of this analysis was to determine how presentations which represented the best practices in client presentations could benefit from the perspective and ideas I wanted to put in this book. If presentations from organizations of this caliber have room for improvement, by extension, so should others.

The goal is show how and where changes might be beneficial. The discussion is also intended to show how presenters might benchmark their own presentations against best practices in two industries, and against what is suggested by an insight-driven persuasive approach. The following are the broad outlines for these presentations:

The new business presentation model for investment manager A

These are key page titles for a current new business presentation created by a successful and highly acclaimed asset manager. The presentation was very polished, professional, and impressive.

- Identification of the client's investment objective or need
- About the manager: guiding principles
- About the manager: characteristics
- What sets manager A apart
- Global research platform: equity, fixed income
- Resources for portfolio managers
- Comparative performance
- Performance highlights
- Private portfolio process
- Client-centered approach
- Working closely with you
- Why work with us

The new business presentation model from the management consulting firm D

This presentation from a major, multinational management consulting firm was also impressive for the same reasons.

- Our understanding.

  Detailed articulation of the client's objectives, as the consultant understands them.

- Our perspective.

  The consultant's thinking about the problem.

  How other clients have approached a similar problem.

  Proprietary research establishing the consultant as a thought-leader.

- Our approach.

  How the consulting firm will go about addressing and solving the client's problem.

- About us.

  Deliverables: what to expect and when.

  Delivery team structure.

  Fees and assumptions

At first glance, the conclusion might be that there is nothing more for a presenter with presentations like these to do or say. But the answer to my question, about whether the perspectives offered in this book could help both the management consulting and investment manager presentations, was yes, and here's why:

- Both could benefit from more focus on the buyer and less on the seller.
- The wide disparity between the actual number of pages devoted to talking about the seller, versus those that talked about how the seller would satisfy the buyer's objectives, showed the clear majority of pages were about the seller.
- Both presentations listed impressive capabilities, but did not take the extra step to link those capabilities to the customer problems they addressed.
- Both presentations could benefit from consolidating the multiple pages of data presented on a single page matrix, or dashboard, or on far fewer pages.

Both written presentations begin with a statement of the client objectives, and both state their commitment to be client-centered in all they do. But after making those assertions, they talk about their capabilities and achievements without tying them to how they would achieve those unique client objectives.

The capabilities and credentials pages could be plugged into any presentation regardless of the client, their distinct goals and motivations, or what it is that they most want to hear from their service provider.

To quantify the customer focus of these presentations, I looked at each page (or slide) in order to do a content analysis of the actual full presentations, not just an examination of the basic outlines shown here. (The actual presentations are proprietary information.)

What I looked for was a clear statement or other explicit indication that the points made on the slide offered a discernible connection to the specific client involved. If content on the slide seemed to be a generic claim that could be applied to any client, I characterized that page that way. On the other hand, if the page featured content that linked directly to the specific client's objectives, I considered that a page with an explicit focus on the particular buyer.

What I found was that 80 percent of the slides in both written presentations were generic, with no discernible link to a specific client or that client's unique objectives. To be clear, these were the written or prepared versions of the presentations. In reality, the delivered presentations may have been much different. The presenters may have drawn links to the specific customer verbally, on the fly.

Nonetheless, the written versions did not include any such verbal asides or conversational extras to help build the case. These written presentation documents are often provided to customers prior to the meeting and always left behind after meetings. When they are sent in advance, there is by definition no voice-over commentary to accompany them. That is why written presentations must *document* the way that sellers claim that their product fits the client. This is a record that the buyer may want to review prior to the meeting and after, when what is said in the delivered presentation fades into memory.

TABLE 3. Buyer-seller focus in state-of-the-art client presentations

Printed slide content	Focused on the buyer	Focused on the seller
Number of pp/slides	8/40	32/40
Percent	20%	80%

This may seem a minor criticism of otherwise high-quality and probably successful presentations, but even these presentations are likely to be less effective without more direct, client-specific connections. You can't create those links by listing standalone attributes in a vacuum. There must be an effort to map your product attributes to the most salient client needs that those attributes satisfy. One of the ways to do this is by employing the relevant evidence matrix described earlier.

Why is doing a better job of linking attributes to clients a needed and useful improvement? The best answer is that customers seem to prefer that approach. As those recent national surveys from Gallup and SalesForce.com indicated, business customers want less of a focus on product claims and price. They want presentations that are relevant and contextual in relationship to their problems. The main point is that you can't be optimally persuasive by talking about your organization's attributes out of the context of the customer problem they solve.

Sequential from premise, to process, to proposition.

What is readily apparent about the two presentations is that they flow from premise to process, to proposal. They both begin with a premise about the customer problem to be solved. Next they proceed to the process, which in each of these cases includes the specific approach to be used to solve the problem, as well as evidence for why this approach will work. Finally, they end with the proposition and the deliverables.

What cannot be determined from the prepared presentations is whether or not the recommended solutions were logical extensions of the premise. That agreement between proposal and premise is what I call a linear presentation.

Ensuring that a presentation is linear is an example of "scientific-method-meets-marketing." It is the way that all marketing presentations should be structured. When I was in advertising, we rejected various creative strategies once we realized that, despite liking them, they did not flow logically from the customer's insight-based premise and resulting creative strategy. Our advertising had to achieve its business purpose not just score on creativity.

Without better knowledge of the client premise for these presentations, I can't comment on whether or not they were linear. But even with that quality as an unknown, any presenter could benchmark their presentations against these actual presentations and benefit from the results to reinforce the good things that you're doing and suggest ways to fine tune them.

I wasn't in search of what might be wrong with these presentations as represented in their written form, but I wanted to see for myself what the state-of-the-presentation-art really looks like today. That said, I would I modify them to make them better in these three ways:

1. Better synchronize the written presentations with the delivered presentations.
2. Avoid jumping on the capabilities bandwagon.
3. View everything in the presentation through a prism of what is relevant to the client.

Synchronizing the written and delivered presentations

The voice-over commentary may be the *only* aspect of the pitch book or PowerPoint presentation that is tailored to a specific client. But the written presentation should also have a degree of customization.

That pitch book may have been sent in advance and the audience will arrive with specific questions. The actual presentation will most always consist largely of answering questions and making specific points to strengthen the case along the way. That is even more reason to put client-specific commentary into each *customized* written document, rather than leave it all to the spoken presentation.

Most road show presentations don't do it that way, but maybe they should. Tailoring written presentations will provide a record of much of the verbal presentation. Customers refer to these documents when the meeting is over and they appreciate the detail.

When you see the custom fork in the presentation road, take it. Going off script is a big part of adapting to your new customer's specific wants and needs, but it all starts with your written presentation. Don't rely solely on your spoken remarks and verbal commentary to tailor the message to your client, do it in written form as well. It is

No one knows what Lincoln actually said at Gettysburg.

About a year ago, I had a chance encounter with the curator of the Lincoln Papers at The Library of Congress. I met her at an exhibition of Abraham Lincoln's handwritten and cut-and-paste versions of The Gettysburg Address, perhaps the most famous speech in all of American history. Yes, it's true: President Lincoln actually sat at his desk, cutting and pasting together his famous speech from various other drafts and versions. Those drafts are now stored in the archives of the Library of Congress and they give us a fascinating glimpse into Lincoln's process, highlighting the fact that even he sometimes went through multiple revisions of the speeches he gave.

The curator told me that no one actually knows for sure what President Lincoln *said* on November 19, 1863. We have a record of the planned *written* speech—all 272 words—but no record of the *delivered* speech exists. No reliable journalistic accounts of what he actually said have ever been found. Lincoln may have tailored his remarks on the fly, adapting them to better suit his audience in that exact time and place, but we have no way of knowing for sure. All we have is the written record of the initial draft.

I think it's safe to say that the words of our presentations— even on our best days—will never be carved into the side of a building for all the world to see, but it's still important to remember that the *written* record is the one that gets left behind.

If you have something important to say in the delivered presentation, put it in the written one as well.

almost always the case that prepared presentations include additional commentary. That commentary should not be excluded just because you think the presenter will cover it when the speech is delivered.

Don't make your "about us" page only about you.

"People are not very keen to know about organizations, because organizations are harder to relate to than people. Don't boast about your company. Tell us about the problems you're solving."

—Chris Anderson, head of TED[37]

Pages and sections with titles like "About Us" or "Capabilities" are notoriously seller focused. The "About Us" page in the management consultant presentation discussed is a clear example. It was actually just that—all about that organization, with little about how certain company attributes were explicitly and relevantly connected to the potential buyer's matter at hand. Merely retitling such slides can program a certain degree of customer-focused relevance into the presentation. Using headings like "Relevant Capabilities," instead of simply "Capabilities," sends a clear message that the seller is intently focused on the specific customer. Titles like "What We Do and How We Can Help" and "About Us and How We Can Meet Your Objectives" also accomplish that goal and set up the presenter's commentary.

I give Raymond James credit for realizing that their credentials should be linked to what they mean to the customer. ("Our 'about us' is really about you."

—Raymond James, 2017[38])

View your presentation through a prism of relevance.

Every slide or point raised should have some discernible link to the buyer need it is meant to address. Table 4 shows questions you can ask about each set of pages in most any persuasive presentation. These questions are about the logic of your presentation and how well it links what it is that you do and propose to do to how that satisfies the client's matter at hand. The questions are meant to suggest ways to fine-tune any presentation to strengthen the product-customer fit.

TABLE 4. Key questions for a relevance audit

Is the client premise based on broad, generic knowledge or specific insights?
Did you confirm or verify your understanding of the client's objectives and expectations before building your presentation? Will you do so again, before starting the presentation?
Is your presentation linear? Does your proposal logically agree with your premise?
Is your "About Us" slide or section solely about your organization? Or are your company's attributes and capabilities explicitly tied to the buyer?
Did you "jump on the capabilities bandwagon" by touting attributes and capabilities that don't have a clear customer link?

Benchmarking against best practices

Benchmark presentations against best practices as represented by the two presentation outlines presented earlier and versus what is suggested by an insight-driven persuasive approach. As you go through this exercise, note the percentage of what you say about yourself, instead of your customer. If you are 80 percent seller-focused and don't adjust that balance in your spoken remarks, you aren't making the kind of relevant connections that enhance persuasion. If you are 80 percent focused on talking about yourself, you're not spending enough time listening to your customer, and therefore losing the opportunity to offer the more contextual solutions that will help you close the sale. When your presentation is significantly over-weighted about your organization, step back, listen more, and shift the balance back to the customer.

TABLE 5. Benchmarking a contemporary new business presentation against a custom-tailored approach

Section	For a tailored-to-the-customer approach
Opening remarks	Do they lay out the logic up front and set the stage for what is to come?
Our understanding	Is this based on insightful knowledge or pulled straight from the RFP? Did they verify that understanding in advance? Was it accurate? Is there anything else they should cover?
Our perspective	Is this analogous to the client's specific matter at hand?
Our approach	Is this generic or client-specific? Why/how does it solve the customer's problem?
About us	Does this say what the organization's attributes mean to the client?
Deliverables/What to expect and when	Is the presentation linear—i.e. Do the "deliverables" logically agree with "our understanding"?
Fees and Assumptions	
Delivery Team Structure	

Sales talks have one objective: making the sale.

Are your audiences as excited to hear the story you have to tell as are the attendees at the Consumer Electronics Show awaiting the next product announcement from a Silicon Valley CEO? Are great TED Talks great because the story is compelling or because the speaking skills have been improved? Probably a bit of both.

Most of what the rest of the world talks about day to day are the basics of how and why their products provide the best match with their customers' needs and, if not, how they can adapt their offering to improve that match. Customers want you to stand up and get to the point in a way that is respectful and relevant to why they invited you to present in the first place. Sales talks are ultimately graded not on style points but results.

The goal of a sales presentation is not to entertain, motivate, or educate—but to match what you offer to what your customers need, and seal the deal.

Clarify your presentation skills priorities.

Author and presentation consultant, Nancy Duarte, suggested that presenters can commit "career suicide" by using presentation materials and presentation software that did not represent the state of the art in the business segment involved.[39] She may be correct. Good design is important, but not as critical as elements like client relevance, customer insights, and successfully adapting to changing circumstances.

Design and professionalism of presentation materials help to give presentations a look and feel consistent with the current best practices for the organization and industry being represented. I made that a priority at Merrill Lynch. Two of the most valuable members of the department I managed were Margaret and Brandon. They were the people most responsible for building our investment performance software and customizing its output for every client presentation my group produced. Among thousands of presentations made, there was not one standard pitch.

Style versus substance issues come up in almost any discussion about presentation effectiveness. Effective presentations have been defined by TED Talks, splashy product announcements from Silicon Valley, innumerable books, web posts, and articles on tips for making better presentations, and even by applications of Zen! All along the way was PowerPoint with its thousands of attendant templates purported to make any presenter and presentation more professional, visually appealing, and ultimately, more successful.

A classic 2001 article about PowerPoint in *The New Yorker* suggested that some PowerPoint presentations could be so slick they "would mask the lack of a firm foundation in the underlying arguments."[40] The same article cited rules for slide construction focused on brevity and avoiding complexity.

One indisputable conclusion about face-to-face presentations is that the use of presentation software is nearly universal. A source from Microsoft quoted in *The New Yorker* article said there were thirty million PowerPoint presentations made each day around the globe.[41] That is not hard to fathom. While no one at Microsoft would confirm that estimate—I called Microsoft to ask them—they directed me to their *Microsoft by the Numbers* web page, which gave numbers.[42] PowerPoint, as of 2017, is on the desktops of a staggering 1.2 *billion* users of Microsoft Office. That amounts to 2.5 percent of users doing something with PowerPoint on a daily basis. The thirty million number seems a bit more plausible.

If there are thirty million PowerPoint presentations made every day, I bet there are nearly that many that violate some rule for slide construction. TED's Rule of Three is based on the view that people can remember three pieces of information well, and after that memory failures take over.[43] One PowerPoint rule was "no more than seven lines per page and seven words per line." Forty-nine words far exceed what TED would suggest.

Though such guidelines may have valid grounding in learning and communication theory, they are not employed in presentations by many leading organizations. In a presentation by a prominent multinational firm, I counted 223 words on a single screen! That result is similar to what I saw when analyzing other current presentations for significant and successful companies. I doubt their transgressions in slide construction hurt any of them; they excelled on the other factors that have greatest impact on presentation success. I tend to doubt that any capable seller ever lost an account just because they put too many words on a slide.

With the availability of presentation software and some design expertise, it is easy to create a polished, visually appealing presentation. Yet the report card on the state-of-the-presentation-art from customers has said little, if anything, about design flaws, and a great deal more about factors such as the lack of client relevance, a lack of insightful knowledge about the buyer's business, and the resulting inability to provide tailored solutions.

Individual and institutional clients are not so easily swayed that they would be influenced by a tastefully and attractively designed document that disagrees with known facts or simply doesn't make sense. An aesthetically appealing presentation will not overcome a badly formed view of your client that says little or nothing about what they want, and expect, to hear from you.

Design critiques, like so many others offering tips for creating better presentations, don't focus enough on the larger issues that explain the variance in presentation success. They certainly don't address the issues buyers believe are most important to them. They don't address how to adapt to what occurs in the meeting room or how to convey, inspire, and earn confidence.

What's the answer? Invest in great design once you have taken the steps to ensure that you have developed the substance to make your case. Resist the tendency to perfect the way you talk about yourself before you have perfected your understanding of your customer. Re-engage your customers and shift the balance back to them.

CHAPTER 7

Surgically Tailor

At some point in any presentation, there needs to be more than a generic explanation of how you—and more specifically, your unique products and services—can solve your customer's problems.

A highly tailored presentation is one in which each aspect of what you say about your firm (and its products) is mapped to the client objective it is meant to address. This is very different than saying: "Here are the things we do and things we do best. We hope they work for you."

Were all aspects of my presentations completely tailored to every client? No. Did the successful ones each contain a level of relevance exemplified by a bespoke process? Yes.

Converting in Kansas

One of my most surgically tailored presentations was a defined contribution investment-only proposal. The defined contribution plan sponsor was a national chain of retail stores headquartered in the Midwest. I was presenting our proposal to replace one of the plan's existing investment options with one of our mutual funds. The incumbent investment product was a domestic growth stock fund in that client's 401(k) plan. That fund was managed by a highly successful and acclaimed asset manager with a superior track record to ours in the equity funds category.

We were in position to make this bid because the client had selected the defined contribution plan group at Merrill Lynch to administer their 401(k) plan. The major portion of profitable, fee-based assets in that plan were in that competitor's mutual fund. Our platform allowed the use of nonproprietary funds, but we couldn't be as profitable on the account without the higher fees that a proprietary fund provides. We needed to have the assets in this competitor's fund in one of our funds.

As you already know or can guess, every bundled 401(k) plan provider wants to maximize the inclusion of their own funds in the plan sponsor's investment menu. In fact, they tend not to allow outside funds at all. Additionally, because of all of the administrative expenses involved, the profitability on assets in defined contribution plans is less than what is derived from more direct-to-the-client mutual fund sales. That was the business reason for our proposal to this new client.

My job, and the focus of my team, was to try to include as high a percentage of our in-house funds in these prospective plans as we could justify. That source of assets and fees was one of the principal reasons that Merrill Lynch had a defined contribution plan business to begin with. Our firm's internal objectives were basically aligned on this point. An account win of this size would be a huge accomplishment and a major source of new assets and fees.

What I said about the fund I was proposing was facilitated by presentation software designed by our information technology person, Brandon. He was an integral member of the investment sales group that I managed at Merrill Lynch, and one of the best people I was fortunate enough to hire. That software was a huge factor in the success of my investment marketing team across hundreds of investment presentations. This was a precisely focused presentation that was facilitated by that software.

What the technology produced was a matrix. At first glance, it looked like a typical fund performance table, but it was a much richer and more versatile presentation device than that. First, it compared the proposed investment—not only to market indices and other benchmarks such as mutual fund category averages and category rankings—but also to a peer group of competitors' products. It included the portfolio characteristics determined to be of greatest importance to the client. They might have been such criteria as risk-return and volatility measures, style consistency, and downside protection, along with manager tenure and experience. It compared our funds to specific competitors' funds on these same attributes. Finally, it was a way to succinctly make the case for an investment option using nearly real-time performance data, not information from prior months or quarters. This information was often current as of the prior day's market close.

Many sources of fund performance data do not have that level of currency. Every investment presentation can and should use a matrix similar in concept, which played a role in this particular client presentation, and in the one to the major telecommunications company described earlier. The evaluative criteria in that matrix were arrayed as reasonably as possible in the order of their known importance to this client. The matrix made a succinct case for why an investment or set of investments best satisfied and fit the client's objectives. It was a tool for coalescing all the arguments in our bid to replace one of their current investment products with one of ours.

With the help of Carl, my associate in the retirement plans group, we asked the client for the opportunity to propose our growth fund as a replacement for their current one. They agreed to give us that chance.

Why would the client do this? In part, for a reduction in their administrative fees. But no plan sponsor would replace a top-performing fund from a noted fund complex for a slight fee reduction. The incumbent fund would have provided fee offsets as well, but as yet had not done so.

One of the reasons the door was open was that this particular client wanted to create the best possible relationship with Merrill Lynch. They were happy with our competitor's fund, and we were not requiring them to replace it, but because of our relationship and the fee offset, they were willing to hear what we had to say.

As you may well know, assets in 401(k) and other pension plans are what we used to call "sticky assets." The managers of employee retirement plans are reluctant to change plan administrators and the specific funds in which their employees invest unless there are very good reasons to do so. Plan sponsors are fiduciaries with obligations for prudent stewardship of employee retirement assets. No plan sponsor wants confused, disgruntled, and worse, disadvantaged plan participants. Therefore, it's very difficult to dislodge (unstick) an existing fund that plan participants and plan sponsors know and like.

Overcoming the buyer's fears

In an excellent commentary about buyer motivations, that team of lecturers at MIT's Sloan School of Management, suggested that one of the key challenges in any sale is overcoming the various fears every buyer has about making the wrong decision—fears that are economic, career, and even social-status driven.[44]

In this case, our client, the plan sponsor's retirement plans director, had definite fears about making the wrong decision. His responsibility was to select investment products that helped (and did not harm) his company, its employees, or his career. There was some personal, reputational risk in this decision. To further heighten these concerns, our proposal was designed to "fix" something that wasn't broken.

This was not going to be an effort to highlight the negatives of the competitor's fund. There were few, if any, shortcomings anyway. If I were to highlight negatives, I would have been calling that client's judgment into question. After all, they selected that fund for their plan. We had to give the client permission to select our fund, and do that with a positive campaign.

When our client agreed to listen to our proposal, he told us that our assignment for the meeting was to demonstrate that his plan participants who'd been investing in the incumbent fund would be at least as well served, and preferably better served, by a Merrill Lynch fund. If he made the decision to select our fund, he would have to defend it with his management team *and* his fellow employees.

The presentation I designed to make the case was:

- transparent and exacting in its detailed comparison of our fund to the incumbent fund on the criteria of greatest relevance and importance to the client.

- not solely based on comparisons to market indices and category benchmarks, but head to head and fund to fund.
- complimentary, not disparaging, of the competitor's fund.
- focused on the factual advantages of our fund, not subjective ones.
- built on what I regarded as the gold mine of information in the mutual fund board report on our own fund, particularly the data on peer group fund comparisons.
- designed to establish parity on the most salient decision criteria and discover aspects of superiority on others.
- specifically tailored to the client's decision criteria, free of boilerplate materials.
- displayed on a one-page matrix.

This was a complex investment story. I wanted to provide the client with a focal point that summarized the relevant evidence that I tailored to fit their matter at hand.

Why this presentation device worked.

As anyone in investment management knows, there is an enormous amount of data on every mutual fund. Portfolios can be compared to benchmark indices on sector allocations, P/E ratios, earnings growth, market cap, and performance attribution from stock and sector selection to name just a few of the possible measures. Individual investors have access to much of this information from one-page Morningstar reports.

Information begins to lose marginal utility when you include too much of it. Not all attributes can be equally meaningful to the client. You need to find a way to pull them through the knothole and make the remainder surgically relevant to the audience.

What I call a Relevant Evidence Matrix as illustrated below is a presentation instrument that accomplishes that goal.

I chose the portfolio characteristics I thought were most important to the client in making their decision and included them in this single-page matrix. You could call this matrix a spreadsheet, a data dashboard, or an executive summary. The point is that this type of presentation device must communicate strong evidence for why you should win by assembling it all in one place and displaying it in a clear, user-friendly manner. This matrix was—and remains—a highly efficient way to illustrate the meaningful differential advantages for why a prospective client should choose your product.

The matrix is not a features chart. It is an array of performance indicators directly related to the attributes of greatest salience to the customer. It is a more powerful tool because it focuses not only on absolute performance and the performance versus benchmarks, but on those criteria—and others—versus actual competitors under consideration.

If your product stacks up well against a competitor, this matrix will clearly show that. Performance shortfalls are apparent as well. Clients appreciate that candor.

If we demonstrated that we had parity with an alternative fund—and the matrix clearly helped do that—our clients were willing to use our in-house fund. If we were at a disadvantage, we didn't gloss over the shortfall. We either conceded that fact, asked to have the fund included anyway, or recommended an outside fund.

Transparency was particularly important in regard to every attribute of our fund, whether that attribute represented an advantage for us or not. When we were able to make that open, objective case for our fund, we had a better chance of giving our client the rationale needed to make the switch. This was not a time to exclude or obscure facts, even if they didn't always work in our favor.

In this case, the client took me at face value. If I had then gone on to say something that contradicted known facts, my credibility would have been shot.

The detail in the matrix

The vertical axis: These are the individual mutual funds being proposed, along with their peer group competitors, category averages, and appropriate market index benchmark or customized benchmark indices.

The horizontal axis: This is the performance across time periods, ending with the most recent possible date for the performance rankings in that category. The data presented often included the most important metrics, such as the Sharpe Ratio and the standard deviation of returns, along with measures of style consistency, downside performance and other portfolio characteristics. The matrix typically also provided information on manager tenure and/or investment experience.

Put competitors in the matrix. The matrix was more persuasive to our clients because we not only benchmarked our funds against category averages, which is what every investment manager routinely does, but also against the performance of funds in their peer group, particularly those we thought might be under our client's consideration. The client is not making a decision to add a category; they are making a decision to select one fund or one fund family over another.

Adding competitors' funds allowed me to control what I wanted to say about how our products stacked up, and not allow a third party such as a pension fund consultant or even social media to have the only role in shaping that dialogue. This was not an effort to disparage competitors, but to provide factual comparisons that the client wanted anyway. The technology we used for this matrix allowed us to import real-time data feeds that made the information current. In fact, we often had year-to-date performance right up to the day prior to the presentation.

Any product can be differentiated from another. The challenge is to find the differences that mean something to the customer. Our fund was at parity on many key attributes, but on others, it had advantages. The key to this takeaway effort was to find ways to differentiate our product that weren't just distinctions, but key differences that meant enough to the client to give them solid justifiable reasons to go to the trouble to make a switch. And we did that.

The matrix was a starting point for a conversation with the client that led to multiple iterations in the presentation. The client asked for other comparisons on key metrics, so I modified the matrix to meet his request. Subsequent changes to the matrix made it a better fit with

Relevant Evidence Matrix

	Annual and cumulative returns	Percentile rankings	Portfolio metrics	Manager tenure/exp
Your fund				
Peer fund A				
Peer fund B				
Category averages				
Indices				

what the client wanted—and a way to support his decision to his management and fellow employees.

The mutual fund board report is a gold mine of potentially meaningful differential advantages.

Every mutual fund board of directors' report shows the performance of a given mutual fund against its peers. That information should help any marketing person make a case for their firm's fund. Commentaries from the fund managers themselves talk about how their management of the fund added value.

A comment from a portfolio manager, which was included in an actual 2016 mutual fund board report: "Over the past six years, the fund's strategy generated a 67.4 percent total return vs. the S&P 500's 46.4 percent, but only incurred 71 percent of the market's risk." This is the kind of product performance insight I would have highlighted to any client for whom risk and return characteristics were important.

One of the ways presenters sell themselves on their investment products is by asking portfolio managers how they distinguish their funds. They are the ones with the best handle on how they stack up against their peers, because their compensation depends, in part, on that relative performance. I drew my own inspiration for confidently marketing our products from regular conversations with portfolio managers. They have a unique perspective on how to position their own funds that is almost always useful.

Ask for the order.

With the final materials in hand, I asked this client for the order by reiterating that his employees would be at least as well served by our fund as they would be with the incumbent, and be better off in several respects. I told him that we would appreciate being included in the plan, and that my firm had the resources, commitment, and people to continue to benefit the employees who invested in our fund. I had the confidence to do that because I had sold myself not just on the strength of our fund, but on the strength of its fit with the objectives set forth by the client. I had provided a tailored solution to exactly what the client asked for.

We won the account. The plan's assets in the incumbent fund were liquidated and reinvested in our fund. It was the largest defined contribution plan investment-only account, with the highest total management fees the firm had ever won. It produced a huge boost in net new profitable assets for the firm.

I received a nice congratulatory phone call from Bob, the head of our equity funds group and chief investment officer. The huge increase in net new assets and fees accounted for by this single account made the then-new president of Merrill Lynch Investment Managers look a bit better to the new CEO of Merrill Lynch.

He seemed to think it was so much easier than raising that amount with fund sales to individual clients. He was in one sense correct. In another he was very wrong. A defined contribution investment-only sale is not an easy sale.

Using a relevant evidence matrix

The matrix was the focal point for bringing a group of individual arguments together that successfully made our case. This kind of matrix is a timeless and useful way to differentiate almost anything. It was an essential and useful presentation device for every investment marketing person on my team. My staff and I regularly made extremely effective use of matrices, with nearly real-time information, because time-frame calculations are so critical in investment management. In fact, many times I was able to make a stronger case for our funds because their one-, three-, and five-year performance *as of the current month-end* was more favorable than the performance ending in the previous month or quarter. That is how time-sensitive some returns can be. We were ahead of our competitors in the design and technology of this matrix, and it was more user-friendly than many comparative investment performance tables. We excelled in our execution of a meaningful and highly communicative sales tool.

Using a matrix as part of your presentation...

✔ gets to the heart of your entire story on a single page,

✔ focuses your presentation on meaningful competitive advantages,

✔ is highly tailored to each specific client,

✔ enables you to highlight your differential advantages versus peers, and

✔ gives you a ticket to the evoked set of products under consideration by creating a comprehensive story that establishes you as a worthy competitor.

Prospects appreciate having information in one efficient table. This sort of analysis can be the "work product" to help you sell yourself. A matrix programs client relevance into any presentation.

I am not suggesting you use the exact format we developed, I suggest that you take the information you provide to make the case for any investment or other financial product and consolidate it in a similar way—a simple, one-page matrix. It is a highly versatile presentation device that works.

CHAPTER 8

Manage the Copresenter-Client Match

I f you have watched the program *Silicon Valley*, you might recall a hilarious episode about making venture capital presentations for the start-up that is the focus of the show. The self-appointed marketing guru of the start-up, Ehrlich, suggested that the way to attract investors was not to just play hard to get, but develop a reverse rapport with them. He orchestrated a plan for each of his copresenters to launch a parade of insults (at the people they should not be insulting). His twisted logic was that any venture capitalist would be impressed with entrepreneurs who were so confident in their product that they could show utter contempt for their investors. The incredulous potential backers were shocked by the behavior of this ragtag group. Of course, their ludicrous strategy failed miserably.

Ensuring a good fit between the seller's people and the client is critical, particularly for investment services, since individual actors—*and their judgment*—is a large part of the delivered product. Both the proposal and the people presenting it need to fit the client.

Sometimes copresenters need to be propped up. The smartest high-technology person may not be comfortable with clients or are reluctant to sell themselves or the client and find marketing awkward. This scenario is played out somewhere every day. It is why the "fuzzies" and their soft-social skills are needed to complement the expertise of the techies. Scott Hartley's book on the need for both capabilities in any business enterprise, *The Fuzzy and the Techie: Why the Liberal Arts Will Rule the Digital World*, makes this point.

So what does the lead presenter do when a copresenter/client fit isn't a good one? How does the presenter make alterations in real time, at the critical moment, when they are desperately needed?

Winter was beginning in the United States. Vance, the head of our tax-exempt bond group, had just received a call from Robert, one of the top financial advisors at our Anchorage, Alaska office. Robert wanted Vance to send a representative to meet with a prominent local family who had just received very substantial proceeds from the sale of their Alaskan grocery store chain to a larger supermarket company headquartered in the "Lower 48." The family, as Robert determined, wanted the majority of their newfound assets to be invested in a portfolio that would provide them with a source of stable tax-free income.

Vance asked me to go along to coordinate the portfolio presentation, which was to be made by Will, one of Vance's newly hired portfolio managers. Will had minimal experience in client presentations. However, Will was intended to be the marketing person for privately managed, tax-exempt bond portfolios. Though he was hired for this role, Vance was concerned about Will's "people/marketing" skills, not his portfolio management capabilities.

It's always good to be asked to do more and to have someone in your company who thinks highly of you. I appreciated Vance's confidence in me and thought it would definitely be an interesting opportunity. He clearly didn't want any feedback from the Anchorage office other than that we'd been prepared and professional with their valued client. It was not only his department's reputational risk at issue. It was the size of the opportunity. This account would likely be the largest separately managed tax-exempt bond portfolio at the firm.

Vance knew that Robert could have just as easily invited an outside manager to make the pitch. Using our in-house portfolio management division was not a requirement. We needed to continually earn the trust of the Merrill Lynch network.

Anchorage is nearly six thousand miles from Princeton, New Jersey, and Merrill Lynch did not pay for business or first-class travel on domestic flights. On the day of our trip to Anchorage, we were on a full flight in a crowded cabin. Almost immediately, my colleague became a bit distressed when his carry-on bag wouldn't fit into the overhead compartment. Any frequent flier knows this type of passenger. He jammed his bag into the space and slammed the bin door shut. Was he likely to be patient, professional, and likable in the meeting the next day? I started to have my doubts.

We arrived in Alaska and woke to a frigid day early the next morning. The seeds of discontent for this portfolio manager had clearly been sewn. The only question, to me, was whether they would manifest during the meeting with the client, or whether he would be able to rise above and be a positive copresenter who related well to this family.

First, we met with Robert to review the client's investment objectives. He told us about which family members would be in attendance and their particular points of view.

The food store chain this family had built was clearly their life's work. Selling it had been an emotional experience. Their income would now be based solely on the investment of proceeds from that sale. Certainly, they weren't going to place those assets with anyone they didn't trust. Fortunately, they trusted Merrill Lynch's local financial advisor. Beyond that however, it was up to us to build on that relationship and demonstrate that Robert had chosen wisely by inviting us to present to his valued client.

Sometimes you can ascertain very pertinent things about a client's worldview from the look and feel of their office environment. This client's offices, for example, were entirely unpretentious. The walls were covered with simple wood paneling. Nothing flashy. No extras. This family's company didn't become successful by wasting money that belonged on their bottom line. They were good judges of people and products and what represented good value. They wanted a conservatively and prudently managed portfolio that would not be a source of stress. Trust and confidence were paramount.

Even before we arrived at the family's offices, Will seemed unhappy about being on the frozen winter landscape. The compelling physical beauty of Alaska was completely lost on him. He lacked a level of enthusiasm that was up to me to replace. Even before he spoke, he seemed to come across to the family as someone who'd rather be somewhere else. At that early stage, it was already clear that the fit just wasn't there.

As he began his discussion of how he would manage the family's portfolio, it became obvious that the fears of his department head were well founded. He was not inspiring trust and confidence. The family representatives were friendly and likable people. This manager was not projecting those qualities, and that was apparent. I doubted that this customer would feel comfortable entrusting their assets to him. That was the bottom-line problem.

It seemed that I had no choice except to step in and refocus the presentation to what I believed was most important to the client. I talked about our firm's long history and experience with tax-exempt bonds and the strength of our offerings. I noted our commitment to client service, including our assurance that we would meet with them in person, in Anchorage, within the first six months and annually after that for a comprehensive review. I focused on the role of the other members of our team, including our highly capable and personable financial advisor in Anchorage.

With this approach, I was taking the edge off this portfolio manager. I made him look good, by saying that he was a member of a very capable organization. The intended customer reaction was not that there were better people than this individual back in Princeton, but that they were talking to the person who would bring substantial resources to bear on their account and that would be of great benefit to them. I was helping to sell Will, because he was not doing a good job of selling himself.

We learned later that day that the family selected us to manage their account. That posture and the way I counterbalanced a counterproductive portfolio manager's presentation were what likely saved the day and won the account. Vance called the president of the asset management group to tell him about our significant account win and the role I had played. The congratulatory phone call I received was one of the best of my career. I appreciated the opportunity to go to Alaska to compete for this account. Our reward was a substantial portfolio, a new valued client, and a new fan in our Anchorage, Alaska, financial advisor.

In the asset management business, you have to appreciate the confidence total strangers put in you. I never took that for granted. The entire experience of getting to Alaska, working with Robert and this client, and ultimately winning the account was one of my favorites. In the end, had we not done a capable job with this proposal, Robert would still have had his relationship with the family, but would have brought in another investment manager. And we might not have heard from him in quite a while.

Propping up copresenters

If you sense that there is a client issue with an individual copresenter, focus on the team, and treat all of the resources of your company as the real product. One way to coach a willing copresenter to relate to clients and not alienate them is to make sure they understand that the rapport they develop with the client may ultimately mean much more than their investment or other expertise in winning an account. You may have to take the ball and prop up those copresenters yourself. Your job is to make them look good. Your client is buying them more than they are buying you. But you have a great deal to do with impression management for the entire team.

The lead presenter as emcee: helping a star fund manager create a personal fit with the client

As we have already seen, one of the roles of the lead presenter is to help copresenters stay on track. Team presentations involve multiple individuals, some of whom are not as adept as others in the way they present and interact with clients. Often these are the same individuals who actually deliver the product to the customer. People like portfolio managers, the people most investors really want to meet.

The presentation in Alaska was partly about compensating for a presenter who didn't develop a good fit with the prospective customer. And that particular individual had an entire team behind him. Now imagine a situation in which that portfolio manager had a nationally recognized performance record. He also had a team, but he was far and away the leader. *He* was the product. It was his strategy, his imprint that had created his track record. He was the person that investors *needed and wanted to meet.* Without confidence in him, investors wouldn't invest. Sometimes a compelling investment story simply isn't enough. Sometimes it's about the players.

The lack of comfort with and confidence in an individual, whether that person is the founder of a start-up, an established CEO, or a star portfolio manager with a new investment product can doom any sale regardless of the other merits of the investment opportunity. That's what happened with the individual who created the urban transportation service business that became a worldwide phenomenon. It could have happened with an acclaimed portfolio manager and a new hedge fund we launched with that manager at the helm.

A distinguished track record is rare and hard to ignore, but investors can't buy the track record. Instead, they are buying the expectation that the individual responsible will continue to produce that kind of stellar performance. Buyers need to be convinced that skill—not luck—produced those returns, and that it can be replicated. In these situations, it all comes down to confidence in an individual, not a system or a team.

You might say that that no investment firm should be so reliant on one individual, but that is the reality for many investment firms, from boutique money managers to hedge funds to major mutual fund companies. When investors like the performance history, the only issue that remains is the person responsible for it. It all comes back to being trusted, believed, and—yes—*liked*. When those elements are missing, for many potential clients it means *no sale*.

Occasionally, the role of the presenter is akin to master of ceremonies. Before the "stars" of the show ever take the stage, the presenter must lay the groundwork in their opening remarks. The presenter introduces the key players and gets the audience predisposed to like them—maybe even excited to hear what those key players have to say.

This is certainly a role that I played many times with Steve, one of our star portfolio managers. Over a multi-year period, the two of us met with prospective clients and investment consultants in the United States, Europe, and China. In fact, when it came to institutional accounts unrelated to defined contribution plans, I spent more time with Steve than I did with any other portfolio manager at Merrill Lynch.

Steve was a former Marine who got his MBA from the University of Chicago. At various points in time, his rolling ten-year track record with a regional international mutual fund at Merrill Lynch made him the top-performing mutual fund manager—in all categories—in the United States. A truly incredible accomplishment.

Steve wasn't the kind of guy to sell potential investors himself. He had no problem explaining what he thought he could achieve and why. He was always confident in his outlook—but he was never one to over-promise. He was almost too self-effacing. He didn't make guarantees. There were times when he seemed not to enjoy the necessity to play a personal role in attracting the investors needed to launch the fund. His mutual fund was sold by mutual find wholesalers and financial advisors with little more than his involvement in a videoconference. Steve was not in our meetings to ask for the order. That was my job.

So what role did I play with Steve and how did I play it? Primarily, it was my job to find the prospective clients who would be interested in hearing about him and the new Pacific Basin hedge fund he was set to manage. I worked through the Merrill Lynch retail network and the capital markets group in the United States and Europe to do that.

Incidentally, I think that Steve would consider our investor meetings in Europe among the most interesting of his career. We spoke to the keep-it-close-to-the-vest Swiss bankers in Geneva, wealthy individuals in Paris, an affluent family patriarch in Lausanne, Switzerland, and European subsidiaries of major US corporations headquartered in England.

I arranged the meetings with leading pension and endowment fund consultants in the United States, and then followed those meetings with the pension and endowment funds themselves. I sent the initial briefing documents and pitch books to everyone involved in an effort to presell the hedge fund and Steve himself. In that sense I played the role of tour manager arranging dates and venues for a rock band. That analogy was not that much of a stretch. Because of his performance record, Steve fit the bill as rock star in the investment management industry.

Once, we got to the meetings themselves, I tried to minimize what I had to say and not detract from what Steve had to say or from the questions our prospective clients raised. Those clients were there to hear him, not me. At the end of the meeting I talked about contract provisions, account minimums, and the two-and-twenty fee structure—the 2 percent management fee plus 20 percent of appreciation. (By the way, this was the fee level that Warren Buffet believes is impossible for hedge fund managers to absorb and still beat the S&P 500.)

The important role for me or anyone in my position to play was not simply to get out of the way. Typically, I would introduce Steve and highlight his track record and his interesting personal history. Once he started his remarks, I usually only spoke to insert gentle reminders about points that I knew he wanted to make or ground that I knew he wanted to cover. I tried to help him build and sustain his rapport with the client.

My message to prospective clients was that they would get a manager with a unique product and a proven, relevant track record who had the expertise and experience in the Pacific Rim to deliver results. This fund's strategy was designed to achieve well-above-market returns. Those were the meaningful, relevant benefits that needed to be conveyed.

Certainly, it helped that was I confident about selling Steve to the Merrill Lynch network. Long before our first meeting together, I had sold myself on Steve and his highly capable team, a fact that came across clearly to our prospective investors. Even so, I knew the personal fit between Steve and our potential clients was of supreme importance. I did everything I could to strengthen that. Marketing Steve was analogous to marketing the founder of the urban transportation service. The decision to invest was more about the principal than their business approach.

Steve had an outstanding "story" product and a long, distinguished record with his international stock portfolio, but he had a limited track record with the new investment strategy he was proposing for this particular hedge fund. Future sales would have to be based on the prospective buyer's confidence in Steve as the fund manager. The case to be made was more about *him* than about the returns he'd generated with other related products. Fortunately, way beyond everything else, Steve was motivated to excel and use his expertise and hard work to achieve superior performance. All I had to do was help him demonstrate that conviction.

Investors want to make good choices and feel confident that they're not making a mistake. They also want to discover and invest with uncommonly talented people who help make them look good. Superstar fund managers like Steve offer a unique product that provides exposure to investment opportunities that investors can't get any other way. Steve wanted investors who appreciated his approach and his expertise. He wanted to work with people who believed he merited their confidence. My job was to help foster that confidence in our investors.

A story fund

The hedge fund that Steve proposed was similar to a *story stock*, only it was a *story fund*. The principal reason to invest in the fund was belief in the portfolio manager, Steve, and less so on the merits of the investment strategy itself. An investor's decision to move forward or remain on the sidelines would be almost entirely dependent on their assessment of the fund manager and their confidence in his ability to do what he was proposing to do.

The basic investment strategy for this hedge fund would be to run an essentially market-neutral portfolio, eliminate market risk, but shift the focus to stock-specific risk. The manager would buy what he deemed to be undervalued stocks in various industries, borrow, and then short sell overvalued stocks in those industries. Returns would be generated by the outperformance of undervalued stocks and the declines of the overvalued ones.

One of the major difficulties in managing this fund was finding sources who would lend the stocks he wanted to sell short. That was because most of stocks would be from Pacific Basin countries. Holders of Japanese stocks, for example, don't want the companies in which they own shares to believe they are dealing with investors who are betting against those companies. Admittedly, there were many special issues and complications in the management of this fund. Nevertheless, it was the kind of unique, alternative investment opportunity that appealed to more sophisticated pension and endowment finds as well as family offices. It was the first hedge fund Merrill Lynch Asset Management had ever launched. Eventually, we attracted investors from each of these groups in a successful launch of the product.

In these situations, the lead presenter's role is to understand that it's investor confidence in the manager and their rapport with the manager that will make or break the sale. They need to explain to the portfolio manager that they have to be sensitive to the particular perspectives in the room. They have to know that the basis for the client's decision is largely their sense of the person. Trust and likability are going to play a significant part in determining the outcome. Understanding that those are key decision criteria has to inform what individuals have to say about themselves and how they say it.

That sounds very subjective but it is the exact presentation skill required in these situations and what I tried to bring to the table. It worked with this hedge fund and with our separately managed accounts with major institutional investors in the United States. I used whatever internal resources I had to take a traditionally retail-driven fund complex and expand its institutional footprint. While I worked with and asked Steve to pursue institutional separate accounts, we established more such client relationships—and they were blue-chip relationships—than we did in any other part of the firm.

CHAPTER 9

Be Constructive Not Contentious

Almost every presentation in every story in this book is about making adjustments in response to what happens in the meeting itself. Many reasons are embedded in these stories for why presenters have to adapt in order to be successfully persuasive.

Reasons you might have to adapt and alter ...

- Presentations just go wrong.
- You misunderstood the buyer's objectives.
- Key decision-makers in the meeting room hold a different point of view.
- The buyer has objections or concerns about your product.
- Challenges are made to your claims.
- Issues emerge with copresenters.
- Your proposal doesn't fit.

What happens in the meeting room can be more important than the substance of the proposition itself in determining the customer's decision. That was the case for every presentation we've discussed. The importance of being able to adapt can't be minimized. It is easy to see how and why the inability to adapt is one of the major reasons that salespeople fail.

So—what skills and techniques are most useful?

One of the most important is preparing to adapt and being vigilant as soon the meeting starts. Sean Watts, a Creighton University law professor, believes that confidence and adaptability are key to success in persuasive presentations. He characterizes a presenter who successfully adapts as one who "continually evaluates a situation and constantly assesses what it calls for."[45]

How to adapt

- If the issue appears to center on a particular individual, support that person but redirect the focus to your company, its resources, and its corporate principles.
- Recalibrate your argument to what is now relevant to the newly defined matter at hand. (Don't give up; and stay in the point.)
- Objections and questions involve retrieving additional relevant evidence or modifying the proposed solution on the spot.
- If you get it wrong, be humble. Make your new case appreciatively yet confidently.
- Always fall back on your belief in your ability to satisfy the customer's matter at hand, even if it's just been modified.
- Don't be defensive. Acknowledge when the client is right; diplomatically set the record straight if they are not.
- Always think about how to be constructive, and never be contentious.

Demeanor determines a lot

Your demeanor in responding to client objections and changing circumstances impacts whether customers trust, believe, and like you.

When you encounter a major objection to your organization or your proposal are you defensive or do you acknowledge the customer's view and constructively address it?

My client in Morristown had a legitimate criticism about the investment performance of our equity mutual funds. I conceded that she was right, but then showed with facts that the individual funds I was recommending to them had strong performance and other characteristics that made them an excellent fit for their plan.

Do you disparage the competition in an effort to make your products look good?

In my presentation to the large national retailer in Kansas, I was proposing substituting our fund for the one they were happy with. If I had focused on the negatives of the competitor's fund, I would have been calling that client's judgment into question. After all, they selected that fund for their plan. I chose the positive campaign.

In Australia, I accepted the blame for getting the client's investment objectives wrong, even though that was because we were given bad guidance from his chief lieutenants. The posture was to concede that it was our mistake, but confidently state that there were many reasons we could not only do better, but turn out to be the best source for the investment strategy that suited his objectives. When it comes to dealing with objections other than obviously baseless ones, there is no point to glossing over your shortcomings or being evasive about your potential customer's legitimate concerns. Every organization has its weaknesses.

When you're under fire for a felony

Presenters can prevail even when facing the most significant problems or objections as long as they acknowledge them in an honest and straightforward manner. Most of those problems, however, likely don't rise to the level of the seller's felony conviction for criminal activity. But even if they do, the same principles apply. Even a problem like that can be successfully addressed and eventually overcome.

So what can you possibly say to potential customers to deal with their concerns about their trust and confidence in your organization after your company's CEO has been convicted of bribing foreign officials? Virtually every RFP contains questions about criminal activity, civil lawsuits, and the like. If you need to check the box next to the question, "Has your firm ever been convicted of a felony?" you have an issue.

This was a real situation for a major global engineering firm headquartered in the US. Even though it had been convicted of this crime and was paying fines to the federal government, it was still a major player and a going concern responsible for some of the biggest, most complicated projects in the world, including much of the rebuilding of the World Trade Center in New York. I know one of principals at this company who was not implicated in the violation. I was curious about his perspective on his company's legal troubles and how they might affect current and prospective clients in the midst of contemplating a relationship with his firm. More specifically, I wanted to know how *he* handles clients' concerns about his organization's past behavior.

What does he *say*? His answer to clients about his firm's illegal activity is simply, "We don't do that anymore." There was no evasiveness or glossing over what his prospective clients already knew. Instead, he cut to the chase, offering them an honest, diplomatic, and entirely sincere answer that they would either accept or reject. Ultimately, either way, this is the answer that most of them needed to hear.

Few presenters have to deal with problems that reach this level of magnitude. Nonetheless, every presenter contends with challenges.

In investment management, marketing people are constantly explaining the reasons certain investment products have not performed in a way that clients were led to believe or hoped they would. Explaining the reasons for these shortfalls is an important part of the job. It's a very serious issue because the clients involved may have lost a portion of their original investment or more than they would have if they'd invested in a better-performing fund instead.

Sometimes, when we had poor performance, we were fired, but usually not right away, and not very often. Most clients are patient enough to see whether the pattern persists. Part of our favorable client retention record was our ability to explain the reasons behind the results. In some cases that definitely meant owning up to mistakes and clearly expressing regret for less-than-satisfactory results.

Even in the world of healthcare, it has been shown that physicians who apologize for mistakes are less likely to be sued for malpractice. The ones who show no remorse and are too proud to concede that, despite their best efforts, they did something wrong and feel bad about it upset their patients/patient's representatives in ways that prompt them to take legal action.[46]

CHAPTER 10

Sell Yourself First

Your own confidence may be the ultimate arbiter of whether a customer selects your organization or some other one. Presentations not delivered in a confident manner are likely dead on arrival. Also true, presenters who are "full of themselves" can kill any sale regardless of the merits of their organization's product. The confidence you exhibit as a presenter and inspire in your audience may be the ultimate arbiter of who wins in a competitive arena in which few products have clear cut superiority on most relevant dimensions. Presentations with the same conclusions or ones audiences have heard before are more persuasive when delivered with conviction and enthusiasm. How you say what you say is more important than what you say. Excelling at how you say what you say comes from having confidence—not overconfidence—in what you are selling.

One of the best ways to foster confidence is by going through the exercise of selling yourself first. This was one of the best bits of advice about persuasive communications I ever received. It was from Edward Block, the former head of all public relations and advertising for AT&T and a member of the Public Relations Hall of Fame. He told me the best way to persuade others is to sell yourself first on what you want others to think and do, and then make it stick.

Mr. Block's point was to look at what you were about to say to convince someone to buy your idea, product, or organization, and ask yourself how strongly *you* believe in that story. If you are wavering, argue it out with yourself. You might enlist the help of internal experts like company engineers, research scientists, product design managers, and portfolio managers to help you. That process and that input will give you more confidence in whatever you are proposing and manifest itself naturally and comfortably in the way you come across to any prospect or audience. If you can't sell yourself, you probably can't sell anyone else. There may only be one aspect of your product that can inspire that kind of conviction, but it may be enough to make a difference between a win and a loss.

A buy side view of confidence is that, after a seller inspires that initial confidence in an investor, the seller still has to earn it. As one former investment management CEO told me, when a company walks away from what brought an investor on board in the first place, any demanding investor will jump ship. What this CEO said reminded me of what Senior Federal District Court Judge Lyle Strom told me when I asked him what he thought made someone persuasive. He said it's a lot about *how* they say what they say—the foundation and first part of confidence. Then, he said, he takes people at face value until they say something that contradicts known facts.

I asked, "How often does that happen in a court of law?"

His immediate answer: "All the time." In his experience, it's that very moment that confidence, once gained, is quickly and irretrievably lost.

It would seem that being honest and straightforward is a given, particularly in a court of law. But that is clearly not the case, and not the case in financial services either, even for assurances made to investors.

Two major examples of companies who failed because they neglected to do what they told their investors they would do: One was an investment manager that lost billions in client assets by not adhering to the commitments they made to their clients. Another was an airline that abruptly changed the business model investors counted on. The airline lost those investors and incurred staggering financial losses as well.

Foster, inspire and earn confidence

The three basic elements of confidence are not mutually exclusive.

The first is the confidence you foster in yourself. The best way to do that is to sell yourself first (ask yourself how you feel about the product and whether it ideally suits this customer) and seek your own inspiration from the producers of the product. In investment management, this might be the portfolio management team, other marketing people, or the senior management of the company.

The second element is the confidence you inspire in your audience, at least initially, through the impressions you create. Generally, this comes from *how* you say what you say. It stems from your conviction and belief in the strength of your product's fit with your customer. It centers on being honest about what you promise and creating realistic expectations, not basing your sale on satisfying unrealistic goals. Inspiring confidence has to do with customers believing, trusting and liking you.

The third component is the confidence you earn, which is through repeated trials, over extended periods of time. The more you deliver on your promises, the more you build confidence and trust. This is sometimes the hardest part, but some sellers make it much harder than it needs to be. Failing to live up to investor expectations they created led to the demise of the two companies featured in the stories in the next chapter.

A presentation that lacks the first two elements of confidence is also headed for failure. In that scenario, the customer sees no point in even giving the presenter's organization the chance to prove they can do what they say they can do. As we saw in the example of the transformational urban transportation company, the most compelling proposition does not always meet with investor approval. That investment opportunity had social proof, urgency, a disruptive technology, and great consumer appeal, and it still failed to attract at least one major investor. What accounted for that loss and many others? Partly, it was the wrong kind of seller confidence, the kind that bordered on presenters being enamored with themselves and their product. That attitude can, on its own, torpedo any proposal.

In the final analysis, perceived quality and satisfaction, with most any service, is primarily a function of expectations and the extent to which they are met. In many ways, at their core, services can be seen as a performance against an agreed-upon set of promises. That pretty much describes what investors are buying when they hire an investment manager or purchase one of their mutual funds. Just as the wrong kind of confidence can lose a sale, the right kind of confidence inspired in the audience can win accounts that would otherwise be lost.

Conveying confidence: When all else failed, being cordial and confident in California

"The skills needed to think quickly on your feet and interact with clients remain uniquely human," according to Scott Hartley.[47] That was the case for me in a presentation when the client was a State Department of Insurance for a very large state in the western United States. The potential assignment involved the management of assets from a failed insurance company that had been seized by that state. The assets were mostly invested in high-yield bonds, a.k.a. "junk bonds," which was the significant reason for the insurer's failure. Not adequately diversified, they failed when the value of those bonds declined.

Ours was a competitive bid. We were pitted against major investment managers from the West Coast and across the country. It was my first institutional asset management presentation since joining Merrill Lynch. I went to this meeting with Alexa, one of our high-yield bond portfolio managers. It happened to be her first institutional client presentation as well. Victor, the senior manager of her group, would have been there but he was unavailable. Thankfully, Alexa was capable, professional, and related well to this client. But Alexa and I had not worked together before.

Almost immediately our presentation got off on the wrong track. What we said was fine, it just didn't seem to me that we said it with the right level of conviction. Things didn't move at the right pace. The presentation was tentative and out of sync. I took the blame for that.

The competitors waiting in the outer hallway wouldn't have this problem. These were savvy, major institutional money managers that had many more institutional high-yield bond clients, and many more institutional clients in general, than we did.

We were about to end our remarks to the committee with the whimper that I knew would fail to produce results. We were not giving this client enough good reasons to choose us. Throughout our choppy presentation, we didn't sound like a major player in high-yield bonds, even though we were. I had to pull our story together and leave a better impression.

I decided to stop worrying about anything that transpired before and ignore my inner critic of our presentation to that point. Instead, I confidently expressed my belief in our ability to effectively manage the assets in question in accord with the insurance department's objectives. I told them we would greatly appreciate the chance to be their investment manager. The *relevant evidence* I used to bolster my enthusiasm was simple: we had an excellent high-yield bond team, including Alexa, that was headed by one of the best and most experienced high-yield bond managers in the country. I had sold myself on the strengths of our high-yield team before this meeting. I was certainly more confident in what I said as a result of doing that.

I focused on client service. I told Rand, the senior insurance commissioner, that we would return regularly to meet them in person to provide reviews of our progress. If they didn't select us, I said emphatically, it wouldn't be because we lacked a major commitment to personal client service for their account. That closing comment was a sales heuristic I borrowed from my colleague Dan, by the way. That attribute, I always felt, was perhaps our major, most-meaningful point of difference versus our competition, and it needed emphasis. More than that, however, the promise of outstanding customer service was an expectation that was under our control. In a business sector in which so much of what we did was characterized by uncertain outcomes, superior customer service was an element of certainty that the client should always be able to count on.

Meanwhile, some of the top institutional asset managers in California and the country were waiting outside the conference room to give their presentations. If they had witnessed ours, no doubt they would have scoffed at our less-than-polished effort. In fact, when we walked by these competitors out in the hall, I had the sinking feeling that we'd already lost the account. I expected one of them to win it. I felt that we were out of their league.

Alexa left in a taxi. I sat on the curb, annoyed with myself, certain I had failed to take advantage of this opportunity. Then I called Terence, the Merrill Lynch financial advisor who had referred the client to us, to give him the post mortem and express my apologies. Before I could start, he congratulated me on the win! He'd just spoken with Rand, the insurance commissioner, who'd expressed his department's enthusiasm for working with us. Incredibly, we'd prevailed against some of the country's top institutional managers on their home turf.

In the end, it turned to be the first large institutional account win for me, and for Alexa who was such a big part of it, since I joined Merrill Lynch. At that time, it was one of the largest separately managed accounts for the firm. Landing that account was a significant plus for my credibility. It wasn't just the size of the account. Despite the tentative start, I was able to play my role and establish a relationship with an important, sophisticated, and very prominent client. That result gave my management team confidence in my ability to professionally represent the firm in high-profile situations. Presentations like these are ultimately graded on results—not on style points.

As long as I continued to deliver, my responsibilities and the resources allocated to me and my department would continue to grow. And they did. This was a pivotal moment. Presentation success had led to sales and career success. Enthusiasm, confidence, and likability overcame our other shortcomings and ultimately won the account. There is no other way to explain the result. I leaned on the most important aspect of what we had to offer to this client. That was the fit between our strongest capabilities and what they sought in an investment manager—expertise and experience in high-yield and a commitment to a high level of personal service.

I set out to convince the client that this meeting would be the beginning of a significant, high-touch relationship. I knew they had to feel confident in our stewardship of these considerable assets. They would be used to help the beneficiaries of the failed insurer, all of whom were already unhappy with the unfortunate turn of events. This was an important element in the selection of an asset management firm. It went beyond performance considerations to confidence and trust. This client—these individuals—were not trained investment professionals, they were regulators. For them, client service and confidence in people they liked and trusted were the most important selection criteria. It was another clear-cut case of the same basic product being preferred for different reasons by a different customer.

For me, this was yet another reason for being grateful for the confidence clients—all people we had just met—showed in us. This particular client relationship evolved into one of the strongest of all our institutional accounts. It proved that when you do what it takes to earn any client's confidence, you can create great client loyalty and great future opportunities as well.

When you excel against expectations: a chance to manage the largest high-yield bond account in the country

Our relationship with this particular state government entity had gotten off to a shaky start. But what followed was excellent client service and a well-managed portfolio. This led to an offer to manage the assets of another failed insurance company. This one was said to be the largest such failure in the history of the insurance industry in the United States. Our firm's ability to satisfy expectations is why we were given this additional, essentially no-bid opportunity. When I told the state insurance commissioners that we would be returning in months or even weeks with a full in-person review of all aspects of the portfolio, it made a difference in their manager selection process. More important than that, however, was scheduling that meeting—and showing up as promised. That may seem incredibly obvious, but we wanted to leave no doubt that we would satisfy our commitment. It also helped that Victor, the senior portfolio manager heading the high-yield department, and his team, were doing an excellent job managing the assets. All of this was confidence earned.

Eventually, the good things we did and the promises we kept led to an invitation to manage that other pool of high-yield bonds—one that exceeded our current account by several billion dollars in value. Remarkably, from that tentative beginning, we were in line be the lead or sole portfolio manager of these assets, the stewards of what would likely be the country's largest privately managed high-yield bond account.

This failed insurance company was tied to Drexel Burnham's high-yield group in Beverly Hills. That company had collapsed when the junk bond market imploded. Someone had to pick up the pieces, not do a fire sale of the assets, and help to make the company's life insurance beneficiaries as whole as possible. I was anxious to deliver the news about our almost-automatic selection to the president of the firm. This would be a monumental account win and testament to what we'd accomplished with such a highly satisfied client.

So what happened? Our chief legal counsel vetoed our accepting the account. He feared that if we didn't perform well with this additional, massive portfolio, we would be front-page news (for all of the wrong reasons), and draw the ire of insurance policy holders who'd already lost so much. He had a reasonable point.

I argued the case but lost. It was disappointing to fail to derive the benefits of our efforts to enhance this client relationship. The irony, to me, is that many of those policy holders likely would have benefited greatly from our role in managing and progressively liquidating those assets in a methodical, prudent manner.

CHAPTER 11

Price Confidently

Confidence impacts the way you price your product. Marketing is about matching your products and services to the customer needs they are intended to satisfy, *at a profit*. The lack of confidence can be costly.

We were competing to manage the 401(k) plan for one of the country's largest retailers. This company employed well over a million people worldwide and was famous for squeezing costs out of every supplier's offering, and for strictly controlling its own expenses as well.

Their headquarters building was Spartan—actually a converted school building. The CEO's office was far from the opulent one our CEO occupied on the 33rd floor of the Merrill Lynch headquarters in the World Financial Center in New York. There was no granite or marble. But there was a lot of fabricated wood paneling of the type seen on the walls of family rooms in 1970s homes.

When he walked by the CEO's very modest office and the crowded floor of simple, bare-bones yet cluttered cubicles, the director of our retirement plans group said that he could not imagine giving up his fancy office to work there. It was a shock to his sensibilities.

There was nothing pretentious about this organization despite their tremendous success. They cut expenses and sought cost efficiencies everywhere. The dozens of salespeople waiting in the lobby to pitch their products to the buyers inside were likely to face a buzz saw cutting into their proposed prices even if they were fortunate to get distribution in this retailer's stores.

Given this potential client and their mindset, we had to decide how to tailor our pitch and price our product, and assess the impact of that price on our profitability. This company had or would have the largest 401(k) plan in the country, at least in terms of the number of participants. It would be a major name to have on our client roster—the biggest new client opportunity in the defined contribution plan world.

If we shared this client's same obsession with cost control, we would have traveled by bus to their headquarters. But we went to the opposite extreme. We took the corporate jet to meet with the client. This was not just any corporate jet. It was a top-of-the-line Gulfstream, the finest corporate airplane on the planet.

On a cold winter day, we approached the snow-covered fields surrounding the airport. I watched out the window as we prepared to land, and thought we were veering away from the runway. That wouldn't happen in modern aviation with a sophisticated airplane, or would it?

It did. The plane landed left of the edge of the landing strip and came to a somewhat soft stop in a snowdrift. The plane was stuck. We deplaned and trudged through the snow to the private terminal. An inauspicious start.

The ground crew towed the plane back near the terminal so that we could get our luggage, laptops, and presentation materials and be on our way to the meeting. Just before I walked into the terminal, I looked back at the sleek Gulfstream, and saw it slowly rolling forward, picking up speed and crashing into one of the tugs that towed planes and baggage carts. The entire left wheel housing, flaps and all, were damaged. The ground crew had secured the wheels of the plane with blocks, but they slipped free on the icy tarmac. This plane was not going anywhere anytime soon. The repair bill would probably exceed the profit we would earn in the first year of managing this client's plan.

During the plane ride, the discussion centered on the mix of inside and outside funds we would recommend. We earned more fee income on our own funds. The more outside funds we used, the greater the shortfall in revenues we would have to recoup. I pushed for our in-house funds for that reason. If our performance on a given fund in a particular category was competitive, I argued strongly to include it because we wanted the in-house assets, and because we had to make a profit to be in the defined contribution plan or any business.

There was also the all-important annual per-participant fee paid by the employer. The fees on the funds were paid by the participant, but administrative costs were the employer's responsibility. For this client, this was a big number because of the size of their employee population. Of course, our cost to administer the plan with that number of employees was high as well.

As an example—not this one exactly—let's say we were talking to an employer with one million employees. Each move of one dollar in the per-participant fee meant one million dollars to the bottom line. It's easy to push a button to make changes in your spreadsheet and your fee proposal. It's another thing to live with the consequences of overpricing (you could lose the account), or underpricing (you could severely impair profitability). So when you are debating moving that fee from $30 to $10 to $8 to $4 or $2, you are making a major management decision.

I succeeded in proposing a strong investment menu that happened to include an overwhelming proportion of our funds, the ones in the categories that would attract the bulk of participants' allocations. The outside funds were specialty funds in noncore investment categories. This investment array was good for the customer and their employees, the asset management group, and Merrill Lynch. The other key variable in the profitability equation was that per-participant fee. The management of our defined contribution plan group had to make the call on that one.

Would we go all out to win this major account? It would be a feather in our cap and add a huge, credible name to our client roster. Were we good enough on the other aspects of our offering to not have to be overly aggressive on price? Would we be at a disadvantage to some other capable competitor if we did not have a significantly lower price than they did?

In other words, did we have to undercut everyone else to win it?

---

*"There are few professional services firms that, when faced
with an opportunity to land a big piece of business, haven't just
dropped their price to make the deal happen."*

—Simon Sinek[48]

It boiled down to whether we had confidence that we could prevail
without a major fee concession. We didn't. The decision was to price at
the extreme low end and hope that the long-term value of the account
and economies of scale would make up for the short-term losses.

It might have been a reasonable business decision, but not one our
competitors would have made. They would have walked before making
that deal. We wanted to make a statement with this account win, and
we lacked a degree of confidence that we could get it on the merits of
the quality of our services. We needed a more confident stance on factors other than price that would meaningfully distinguish us from our
competition, and we did not have that.

Nevertheless, the decision was made. Our pricing strategy succeeded in one respect. The next day we learned that we had won the
account. The firm had to send another much-less luxurious private
plane to return us to New Jersey. The Gulfstream was still on the tarmac waiting for the arrival of the repair crew from the manufacturer's
home in Savannah, Georgia. The damaged jet was a bit of a reminder
of a somewhat incomplete victory.

Announcing the win

Stan, the director of our employee retirement services group, and I
met with John L., the number-two executive at Merrill Lynch, to tell
him about the outcome of this highly important and visible presentation. We told him about the win. It was meant to be a triumphant, congratulatory moment. The firm wanted account wins with prominent
clients, and we had just won one such account. The senior executive's
lighthearted but serious reaction was exactly this: "Are we going to

make any money, or is it just for bragging rights?" There was some wind taken out of the sails. If the profitability was there, the accolades would have been there.

The takeaway

Confidence plays a role in so many decisions—internal and external. I think if we had a bit more insightful knowledge of how sensitive our client was to price for this service (we knew they were obsessive on cutting costs for virtually everything else), we might have made a different decision. We should have known that we were way under our competitors on the bid. If we had been more confident and enthusiastic in asking for the order we might have won the account with a less substantial haircut on fees.

Pricing is a bit about fear of failure. It may be mostly about that. When that fear takes over, you will drop the price to almost any level in order to avoid losing a major account and the prestige and maybe long-term profit it might produce.

On the other hand, the more that you have sold yourself on the value of what you offer, the more likely you will be to make a winning case for your product that does not rely on price. At least, you can argue your case for the value embedded in your price with your client. If they like your services but don't like the price, you can have a dialogue. We priced this account at such a low point that we precluded that option.

We missed a chance to make our case to this client for why a higher fee would be justified—mostly because we did not believe we had a level of service quality equal to or better than that of our competitors. We had not sold ourselves on what we had achieved and could achieve in this business. There were other seeds of self-doubt that entered the equation. Our competitors had more highly satisfied referenceable clients than we did.

So let's say that we had opted for higher fees. We would be faced with the same challenge as any seller that priced its services 20 percent, 30 percent or 40 percent more than a competitor. You still need to justify why you merit the higher price. We never gave ourselves the chance to make that case. The fact that we won the account told me this client did believe that we had a quality product with capable people. I don't think we ever gave ourselves credit for that. Ironically, they had more confidence in us than we seemed to have in ourselves.

Despite the client's frugal reputation, I doubt they would have selected us for their plan if we didn't have all of the components necessary to be an exemplary provider of employee retirement plan services.

So what else can you say other than that you are worth it when it comes to charging a higher price? One of the first things is to determine what assumptions the client is making about competitors and their pricing. I don't think it's ever good to disparage the competition, but if they are quoting prices that are not reflective of their actual fees over the life of a project, you need to set the record straight. Damning with faint praise may be the strategy. When a competitor is undercutting your price, only to raise it later due to things like production delays, a comment like, "Acme *sometimes* succeeds in meeting their price and timing deliverables," seems fair.

The flipside of this story is that, as a team, we had prevailed against the top competitors in the financial services industry in securing this account from one of America's biggest companies. Its business extended to every state and community, and its brand was a household word.

We were providing a service that would help improve the financial future of its hundreds of thousands of employees. It was a true Wall Street-to-Main Street moment for Merrill Lynch. When it comes to corporate missions, that was a pretty gratifying one to fulfill.

Still we were dealing with a unique company with a unique population of employees. Later in the relationship, we had to understand the ways those employees invested in their 401(k) plans. That was another matter. But let us just say that for many of those employees, the 401(k) was a Christmas-club-like savings account that they would liquidate—even with a penalty—at the end of the year. We made efforts to discourage that investment behavior and alter some investment choices so that employees did not exacerbate the lost retirement savings by selecting investments with higher near-term risk. That employee education function was the kind of added-value service that clients like this one needed, and would have been part of our rationale in our argument for a higher price.

Still, this account represented a big win on the investment side. It was satisfying to me because this demanding client selected all of the funds I recommended. I had to make the case for our internal funds not just with this client, but also with my counterparts in a separate division of the company. I considered it two-pronged victory for my group and me.

That said, this was a team effort and our funds were only part of the story. The clear reason we won the account was the administrative envelope Merrill Lynch created that allowed the enclosure of our investment products. Working with the group financial services division was at times a challenging internal sale, but always a productive one for asset management and the firm.

For me and the team of thirty investment professionals I managed, working with our very capable partners in the defined contribution plan group was, by far, the most significant way we contributed to Merrill Lynch. The assets we helped attract in our productive partnership with them were sometimes the highest source of net new money in our asset management organization. Many of my major account wins and my staff's successes were attributable to working as a team with individuals in groups like this one throughout Merrill Lynch.

I said at the beginning of the book, that the way you present has major implications for your internal status and advancement. It is not only your external audience evaluating you, it is your internal audience as well.

Our internal audience wanted us to help them build their business. And that all started with the broadly insightful view of our external audience and their constituents and proving that we offered the best way to satisfy key objectives for all of these groups. We had to create the best overall fit to win, and we accomplished that.

Conclusions about three elements of confidence

- Foster confidence by selling yourself first.
- Inspire confidence with your faith in the strength of the product's fit with the customer
- —Earn confidence by fulfilling—and not forgetting—the realistic, agreed-upon expectations you create.

CHAPTER 12

Fulfill the Expectations You Create

Confidence and trust are fragile commodities. The soft skills required to establish these qualities need to be followed by actions. If actions are not consistent with expectations created, the business impact can be monumental. Setting realistic and mutually agreed-to expectations is part of every new business presentation. The expectations could be income on assets, or completion dates for construction projects, or enterprise software installations. What you say in the initial presentation fades in importance. It is now what you do that counts.

What is amazing, when commitments are violated, is how costly those violations can be.

A tale of two airlines

One of several new start-up airlines in the United States got off to a very promising beginning. The formula was to fly out of secondary terminals in major hubs, such as the North Terminal at Newark airport, and land at regional airports near major cities. The airline would fly from Newark, for example, to Fort Lauderdale, Florida, but not Miami. Avoiding major hubs resulted in major cost savings versus major carriers.

Additionally, customers gave up certain things like assigned seats and checked bags. There was no complimentary meal service while on board, but you could buy food before you got on the plane. These days, all of that may seem pretty normal, even with a major carrier, but at the time it was well out of the norm. Yet passengers flocked to this airline for inexpensive, no-frills travel. Vacation weekends suddenly became an extremely affordable proposition. And passengers actually liked the minimalist service platform and thought the muffins they could buy en route were actually more appetizing than typical airline breakfasts. Major investors liked the company, the business model, and the stock.

That changed when the CEO made a sudden and unexpected decision that set off alarm bells for at least one of the company's major shareholders. Contrary to his company's corporate strategy and industry niche—the CEO announced that his airline would add some major hubs to its routes, flying right into the teeth of competition from the country's biggest carriers.

The equity analyst in charge at an asset management firm that was significantly invested in the stock was not happy with the news. He confronted the CEO about this change to the business plan which he felt violated the assurances he'd been given and were the basis for the investment in the company.

The CEO stood by his decision to make that bold departure from what had made his airline successful. It still seemed to the equity analyst to be a formula for disaster. This was not why his firm signed on with the company. He exited the stock.

The airline proceeded with its new strategy, igniting fierce price-matching skirmishes with established carriers who needed to protect their turf. Quickly, the airline's customer advantage evaporated and so did their profitability. Soon after, the airline failed. I don't think I've ever heard a better example of an organization losing confidence by failing to adhere to the very clear expectations it created.

Another airline with a similar business model still operates today. That carrier is Southwest Airlines, which stuck to its knitting and has been a top-performing company—and stock—for decades.

Creating realistic expectations and meeting them are important for not only start-ups and story stocks, but for most any investment product. In attracting clients, persuasion is about creating mutually agreed-upon and realistic expectations. It is also about providing evidence that you can fulfill those expectations. That seems so straightforward—in order to retain clients, you need to live up to your commitments.

That is why it seems even more incredible when organizations can control their ability to do what they say they are going to do, and they know that customers and investors count on that, they still fail to do so. It is certainly easier to adhere to a business plan than produce higher stock prices or promised investment returns in markets you can't control. In any case, when it comes to earning trust and confidence, actions speak for themselves.

A fund manager that forgot its customers

If you are not convinced of the fragility of customer trust and confidence or think that the story about the airline that changed course disastrously was a one-of-a-kind case history about a corporate blunder, consider the story of a well-known, New England-based fund manager that lost billions in shareholder value and eventually billions more in asset outflows as a result of violating that trust.[49]

As I suggested in Chapter One, every firm has a stated commitment to be customer-centered. But not every firm has the commitment to do what it takes to be continually customer-centered. The firm that lost its way and so much of its asset base told its clients the following: "Our truth-in-lending approach ensures that we adhere to every fund's stated objective, style, and risk position."[50]

Just for perspective and as a reminder…

✔ The NASDAQ composite hit 5,000 just before the year 2000.
✔ It dropped to about 1,200 in 2002, a 75-percent decline.
✔ It took until 2015 for the index to recover from its precollapse level.

This firm violated that promise by turning diversified mutual funds into highly concentrated and much higher risk investment vehicles than their shareholders wanted. Two of its largest and most successful mutual funds were required by their prospectuses to invest no more than 25 percent of fund assets in a single sector. But in an effort to take advantage of a temporary surge in technology stocks, those funds suddenly had 50–60 percent of the assets invested in that "space," using the common vernacular at that time. When the dot-com bubble burst at the start of the millennium, those funds and their shareholders had devastating losses.

"They forgot the customer."

—CEO of a fund management company that was the recipient of the outflows when a competitor failed to fulfill its obligations to its shareholders

---

To make matters worse, that fund manager started entirely new funds with virtually 100 percent exposure to technology.

To be fair, this firm was not the only one to rush concentrated and technology sector funds into the market. Those "flavor of the day" products were aggressively pushed to financial advisors and their clients without concern for injury to investors who were buying shares at top-of-the-market valuations.

This particular investment manager's actions were extreme. The resulting losses in shareholder value were monumental. They resulted in massive defections from its products by financial advisors and their clients who were the ultimate investors in the investment manager's funds.

This was a vivid example of seeking sales and profits without adhering to corporate principles. This organization got the sequence wrong. The correct order for them and virtually every other enterprise can be summarized by what Dr. Thomas Frist, Sr., founder of Hospital

Corporation of America, once told me: "When you manage the values, the numbers take care of themselves."

Summary and takeaways

Almost any investment advisor would suggest that you take great care in setting expectations because those are the standards by which you will be judged.

Create expectations that are realistic. If the client wants more than you can deliver, it might be wise to decline. If you fail to meet expectations, the client is not likely to be happy, even if you told them that it would be a stretch to meet their goals.

Being realistic in investment management means, for example, not promising that a value strategy will have strong near-term performance when price-earnings multiples are historically too high to justify a major entry point—or that you can produce high current income if the yields are not there to support it.

Whatever expectations you create, adhere to them. Clients and most investment managers who invest on their behalf want the people they rely on to be true to what they say.

If a company CEO or portfolio manager makes decisions that are clearly at odds with their client's expectations, they risk losing investors on that basis alone. Investors want to be assured about adherence to business models and investment disciplines, even though guarantees about increases in the company's stock price or other performance metrics cannot be given. At the very least, the investor needs to know that you will actually *do* what you say you will do.

CHAPTER 13

Use Research to Create the Perfect Pitch

Without data all you have is an opinion. With it, you have insights every audience appreciates. Data can be a powerful ally in successful persuasive communications. Consumer research was the foundation for all creative strategy decisions when I was in advertising, and it continued to play a role when I was in investment management.

Sometimes it is worthwhile to take the initiative to conduct research about your client's issues with their business. There are other ways to provide added-value perspective. Many sellers—particularly professional services and high technology services providers—offer case histories about what worked for other clients in similar situations. But proprietary survey research can be a uniquely powerful source of insights that most all clients appreciate. It can help you help your customers achieve their business-building goals and, in doing so, strengthen your ability to provide solutions that best suit their needs, set yourself apart from the competition, and seal the deal.

Customers appreciate the help that sellers can give them in managing their relationships with their own audiences. Every customer pays attention to data. Data enhances your credibility, takes you out of the realm of offering your opinions, and places you in the position of providing insights that every audience values.

Data can help you create the perfect pitch.

In order to understand and help your customer, you need to know at least some of the challenges and issues they face with their constituents—their customers and employees, regulators, local governments, suppliers, and the general public. For many organizations that sell to other organizations, their audience is their direct customer and that customer's customers.

This is definitely the case for advertising agencies. It's a big reason they employ proprietary consumer research to understand the target consumers for the advertising that they create. The paying client may be Procter & Gamble, for example, but the ultimate audience is the buyer of the detergents, razor blades, and shampoos that P&G sells. This is also true for human capital consultants who help their clients with employee engagement and motivation issues. As such, they require an understanding of employees in similar populations, and likely the specific client organization itself.

Mutual fund companies also have multiple audiences. One is their corporate clients who select the funds that are included in their 401(k) plans. Another one is the participants in the plan who allocate their retirement assets to those funds. Other audience members include the financial planners and financial advisors who sell mutual funds to their clients.

In my advertising and investment sales careers, what we knew about the consumers of our client's product or their employees often distinguished us from our competitors and helped us make the sale. Using survey research insights to help their clients help themselves is vintage added value for advertising agencies and management consultants. It is an idea not lost on financial services firms. For example, many of them have commissioned surveys to help their own sales and marketing people and their intermediaries better understand the investment attitudes and behavior of millennials and other generational, demographic, and psychographic market segments.

Recognize and reinforce the role of using research to improve the overall match between products, customers, and those customers' stakeholders. This kind of information fits with what customers and financial intermediaries want and need from sellers.

"B2B companies that seek to deliver effective advice and drive organic growth need to expand their knowledge of both their customer and their customer's customers."[51]

—The Gallup Organization, 2016

Insights are a two-way street

As the seller, you want insights about your client to help you best suit their needs. Clients want much more than a mere discussion of product and price. They want and need research insights and other forms of added value to help them build their business and/or better serve their existing customers or employees. If there is such a thing as a presentation that perfectly satisfied those goals, one I am about to describe is pretty close to being it. This approach can be just as successful today as when I first used it. Something like it can work for you.

My most significant client relationship during the time I spent in advertising was with AT&T. In fact, before it was broken up into multiple regional companies, AT&T was one of the largest advertisers in the country. At the time, Young & Rubicam managed one small piece of AT&T's advertising budget and was invited to bid on another, which offered huge, fee-based revenue potential. This was an era in which other companies were taking market share from AT&T's long distance business, fueled by court decisions that allowed these smaller companies to tie into AT&T's network and resell that access at reduced prices. AT&T was, in essence, prohibited from either fully pricing that access or undercutting those competitors on price. They were caught somewhere in the middle. AT&T had no choice but to seek other ways to differentiate their services in order to retain their best customers.

The restrictions AT&T faced as the dominant player in the industry might be likened to a court forcing Apple to offer competitors' smart phones for sale in their own branded stores, without assessing costs to those competitors for using Apple's distribution channel. Apple's infrastructure—the storefront, lights, sales staff, etc.—would be free to the new low-cost providers, giving them a massive edge on price.

AT&T had explored various nonfinancial consumer incentives. One was a donation to charity on behalf of the customer. The question AT&T needed answered was this: would their customers see such a donation to be a benefit of using AT&T's services? AT&T's ingoing judgment was that it would be perceived that way, but they had no research we were aware of to support that view. Even if that strategy lacked consumer appeal, few other nonfinancial incentives had been contemplated. AT&T invited its advertising agencies to provide their thoughts on the dilemma.

At that time, I was a member of the new business team at Y&R and managed our research efforts. This was a competitive pitch for the premier client in the category. In fact, it had the potential to transform the AT&T account from one of the smallest at the agency to one of the largest and most important. In this case, the president of Y&R elected to be our lead presenter. He seldom left the office for new business presentations, but he decided to travel to AT&T's sprawling world headquarters in Basking Ridge, New Jersey, for this one. His presence called for an extra effort. He was now in the audience.

This was another case of presentation skills having sales and career impact. I wanted the presentation to work for the client, and for the agency's president, and for the agency to look good in the process. Of course, we could have simply proposed an advertising campaign that fit, in our view, with AT&T's overall charitable donation strategy. However, we wanted to do more. We wanted to discover consumer insights that would help strengthen the customer relevance of our advertising proposal. This required more than our professional opinions and focus groups.

I convinced my boss, John, or he convinced me, to get the agency to hire a major research organization to do a national survey of AT&T's long-distance customers. We wanted data that would be representative of the target audience as a whole. This study was more costly than focus groups, but we wanted the level of validity that a scientifically designed survey would provide.

The survey measured the appeal of donating to a charity as a benefit of using the AT&T's services. We also wanted to learn whether there were particular charities that respondents strongly preferred over others.

We not only found that the idea of charitable donations was favorably received, we also discovered that—of the many possible charitable organizations to which donations could be made—survey respondents strongly preferred the Special Olympics over all others. Very few people did not view it as a worthy cause.

The study was a home run. It not only demonstrated to AT&T that the idea of charitable donations had merit, but provided a unique direction for how to execute the strategy as well. This compelling insight could only have been obtained with results of a nationally representative sample of AT&T's long-distance customers.

A perfect fit

Our proactive research effort allowed us to make a highly credible link between the creative strategy we recommended and the beliefs and preferences the client already held about the charitable donation strategy. They wanted and needed this kind of solution, and we provided the relevant evidence to show that our campaign did that.

AT&T was very happy with our presentation. The president of Y&R was happy with the presentation and even happier about the possibilities it created for substantial and growing billings. He accepted the accolades from Kay, the worldwide director of advertising at AT&T. In her position, she was one of the most powerful people in the advertising world.

We'd succeeded in augmenting the original strategy, which was great, but we'd also positioned ourselves as uniquely qualified to execute that strategy. Of course, even that didn't guarantee that we would win the account—but we did.

What we learned in the research process above became the foundation on which the creative campaign was built. High-quality research creates a degree of credibility that few advertising opinions can match.

And it demands attention. I doubt that any of the competing agencies had taken that kind of initiative to seek objective, evidence-based support for their proposal. Given the precise relevance of our presentation and the strength of our support, I don't believe that our competitors stood a chance of winning the assignment. It was an ideal, perfectly tailored presentation.

Note: AT&T continued to make donations to the Special Olympics on behalf of its customers as recently as 2015.

Why this presentation epitomized an ideal custom-tailored approach

It was based on insightful knowledge about the client's unique challenges. We verified our understanding of the client's concerns and business objectives.

Our relevantly connected proposal was based on the unique and meaningful insights that we'd developed specifically for this client. Our proposed solution was more relevantly connected to the client's matter at hand because it employed proprietary information that no one else had acquired. Our competitors didn't have the basis to know or understand the true value of charitable contributions to AT&T's customers or that the Special Olympics, in particular, had such widespread appeal.

The proposal was confident for the right reasons. We had a research-based rationale on which to base our creative approach.

The proposal enhanced the customer's fit with its audience. At our own expense, we created a research study that offered compelling insights about our client's customers that were directly related to the business challenges that AT&T faced. Those insights became the driver, shaping virtually every facet of our presentation, resulting in a proposal that helped our client and helped our business as well.

A trusted advisor

Our research gave us credibility and made us a trusted advisor. We did the right thing for this client. Being selected for the account was just the derivative outcome of that holistic effort to tailor our proposal to suit the client's specific needs. We did everything the 2016 Gallup survey suggested that business customers seek from sellers. It was an ideally bespoke presentation that created a perfect fit with our client.

These kinds of outcomes are available to anyone who chooses to use survey research in this manner. Talk to a high-quality research organization to see how they might help you help your customers by better understanding your client's constituent groups, including their own customers and employees.

CHAPTER 14

Understand Your Ultimate Client

The experience with AT&T was the catalyst for a similar study designed to help our clients understand their employees and their investment motivations. In this case, our primary clients were the defined contribution plan sponsors who included our funds in their 401(k) plan investment menus, but the ultimate customers were the plan participants that allocated their plan assets to our funds.

"Our conclusion is that short-term changes in the marketplace are driving people to make changes in their plan. It is not the long-term focus we think 401(k) plan participants should have with their retirement money." I made that comment based on a study we did to determine the expectations of 401(k) plan participants for future investment returns, attitudes toward different mutual fund options, and reasons why they made changes in their investment allocations to name a few of the topics. The reason for the study was to provide useful insights to our clients.

Denice was a senior manager for the defined contribution plan business at Merrill Lynch. Her group hosted an annual conference for all our plan sponsors. Her client service director, Mary, wanted to do something different as a centerpiece of the conference, and it had to do with investments.

Instead of providing the asset management group's investment or economic outlook—often not the most exciting material for a group like this, I suggested that we pay for our own national survey of 401(k) plan participants. The study would be focused on plan participants' attitudes toward investing for retirement. We did a companion survey of our plan sponsors so we could compare the perceptions of the two groups.

I hired a nationally recognized firm to conduct the survey. I wanted to use a respected and broadly experienced research firm because we wanted our clients to have confidence in the external validity of the results. We also wanted to give them something they would find uniquely interesting to take home and use in making their 401(k) investment menu decisions.

A scientifically designed survey managed by a quality firm controls the sample bias inherent in voluntary surveys such as the online ones that have become so common. Respondents to voluntary surveys are the ones who feel most strongly about issues one way or the other, and include very few of those who fall in between.

Many voluntary surveys start with a universe that is already biased. Voluntary viewer polls by television news networks are particularly biased because their viewers tend to cluster at one end of the political spectrum. We wanted unbiased results that could be projected to the larger universe. For this study, the universe was individuals in corporate defined contribution plans nationwide.

This turned out to be one of the most interesting national surveys I ever did. The results were surprising. Our plan sponsor clients agreed. The presentation managed to maintain the attention span of people who were looking to end the morning session and enjoy the amenities of the resort hotel in Scottsdale.

That presentation was a highlight of the meeting, and here is why: The study showed that investor expectations for future stock market returns had exceeded anything close to the reality of long-term returns in the US and foreign equity markets. These retirement plan participants were reacting to recent experience in the markets, which produced 30 percent, 40 percent, and even higher annualized returns in short periods of time. That euphoria was due to the infamous technology bubble that drove the NASDAQ index to historic highs in the years up to mid-2001. In 1999, the stock market finished up by 21 percent.

Against that backdrop, over 71 percent of respondents in our survey expected the annual returns in the stock market to exceed 17 percent over the next five years. In contrast, plan sponsors expected returns of 10–12 percent per year going forward. Both of those forecasts exceeded the historically 7–8 percent annual real returns generated in the stock market.

What surprised plan sponsors was the wide disparity of expectations between them and their participants. Nonetheless, the predictions from both groups were way off. For the five years from 2000 to 2005 the S&P 500 declined at a compound rate of -1.12 percent per year.

Our clients left the meeting thinking they learned something new and relevant to their jobs, and that definitely helped to make the trip worthwhile. It wasn't just our opinion about what was happening in their world, it was a valuable insight from a national poll, and evidence that was directly related to their fiduciary responsibilities to provide reasonable and diversified investment alternatives for their employees.

This research led many plan sponsors—now alarmed at the unrealistic expectations of their employees, and maybe their own as well—to reassess their investment menus. Their DC plan participants were clearly reacting to the prevailing market conditions. Over 35 percent of plan participants wanted Internet and technology funds added to their 401(k) plans. Those requests were driven almost completely by recent short-term returns.

Our own data showed that nearly 90 percent of plan participants made annual changes in their investment selections during the time of the technology bubble. That compared to 26 percent making those changes in the two years before. The reason participants gave for the changes was their view of the prospect of lofty returns by switching from funds with good recent performance to others with even better performance.

Several sponsors removed—or at least elected not to add—highly volatile single-sector mutual funds, like technology funds, which were fueled by the 2001 dot-com bubble and collapsed when it burst. The survey results gave them highly relevant insights that altered their decisions.

Individual investors were not the only ones chasing performance. As any investment firm person who lived through that period knows, many mutual fund managers, including Merrill Lynch, were quick to bring new Internet mutual funds to the market.

Participants react strongly to market performance when making allocation and investment decisions. According to an IBM survey of its 401(k) plan participants done at the same time as our study, "The most important attribute of an investment option is performance, with 96 percent rating it very or somewhat important."[52]

The study and the actual aftermath of what happened in the collapse of NASDAQ, were warning signs about the dangers of flavor-of-the-day investments for retirement portfolios. The demise of defined benefit plans and the transition to defined contribution took control over investments from professional investors and put it in the less-experienced hands of individuals. That transition still left plan sponsors with the responsibility of prudent stewardship of the investment options offered and how employees allocated their contributions. That also meant helping to save their participants from making decisions that were clearly not in their best interests.

Implications and takeaways

This particular example illustrates the benefits of data and how it can help to frame or augment customer objectives. Anyone can use research insights and other insights to help customers find better ways to meet those objectives. Data takes presenters out of the mode of offering only their opinions and capabilities as evidence. In fact, providing relatable research to prospective clients is almost always appreciated. It may add a meaningful point of difference to any recommendation.

The results of the Gallup survey of business customers showed that buyers want more than just product and price discussions in their interactions with sellers. They want sellers to give them insights and advice that relate to their business and business-building efforts. Research studies are one way to do that.

Institutional and other clients want to know what similar clients with similar objectives are doing. This is a common request made by defined contribution clients, too. They are always interested in what specific investment options other companies have included in the investment menus for their plan participants.

Just as customers want advice from a salesperson, or their tailor, about what fits them best, plan sponsors also want feedback and reassurances that their investment menu allows their participants to satisfy their unique, individual investment objectives. Those objectives can vary widely according to the participant's age, years to retirement, and risk tolerance. All are obvious factors to anyone in the mutual funds industry.

If you are recommending an investment menu to a client, one of the ways to persuade them to accept your recommendation is to talk about how and why other clients have taken a similar approach. Perspectives about what other clients do are a credible adjunct to your own view as an investment management marketing person.

In almost every one of my 401(k) plan investment presentations, I tried to add a section about what other clients were doing and explain the rationale for my recommendations. Of course, not all of those clients may have been doing what made sense generally or specifically for some other plan sponsor. It was another view and they looked to people like me to provide it. This is about providing a perspective based on data, not opinion or a range of experience.

Funding research that your clients can use is almost always a great idea—for supporting evidence and other reasons. It gives them the opportunity to obtain independent information pertaining to their customers, employees, or competitors. And it takes you, as a presenter, out of the realm of just offering your opinions.

Regardless of the size of your firm or client base, there may be cost-effective ways to obtain this data. I encourage anyone to seek out ways to do that.

A word about research methods

It is often worth the investment to commission high-quality survey research because it can provide more projectable results and give your clients a firmer, more objective basis for taking any action that depends on that kind of information. Lower-grade research—specifically the ubiquitous voluntary online surveys so often used today—simply can't do that, and no one should encourage an audience to believe they can.

"Qualitative research," the term used here for focus groups and small-sample or one-on-one interviews, is not the same as high-quality research. The term mostly means that the results of the research have to be *qualified*. That is not to say that there isn't good or insightful information that can flow from focus groups. It just means that any conclusions need scrutiny.

You can obtain some directional information from focus groups, which can be very useful for certain purposes. I would place voluntary online surveys in the same category.

When I worked in advertising, I spent an enormous amount of time designing and attending focus groups. I couldn't have done my job without them, but I learned how to discern what made sense, what seemed reasonable, and even what proved insightful. Focus groups can be a great research tool, and in many cases are preferable to having no research at all, but you have to be careful about how far to go with conclusions drawn from this source.

I evaluated focus group findings this way. I attached greatest importance to feedback that was spontaneous, consistent within groups, across groups in the same city, and also across groups in different cities. If a comment or concern met those standards, I felt better about its potential importance to our product development or advertising efforts.

High-quality survey research produces a level of confidence that can't be achieved with qualitative research or voluntary surveys taken by mail or online. If you or your client are going to base business decisions on research results, it is worthwhile to have results you can count on. Having a large sample size for a voluntary survey—for example, thousands of respondents—means very little. It all depends on the universe from which the sample was taken, the response rate, and the response effects due to the wording of questions.

These surveys always sound impressive. It is just impossible to know—without understanding their methodology—that anything they conclude is valid in the larger population. There is no "A" for effort here. If you feel that survey research can help you discover insights about your client and your client's constituents, it's worth the effort and expense to conduct a scientifically designed survey.

Closing phrases and sales heuristics

One example of such phrases or heuristics is the classic statement uttered by CEO and spokesperson, Lee Iacocca, in an advertising campaign for Chrysler, which under Iacocca's stewardship was emerging from bankruptcy and heavily focused on the quality of the cars it produced. At the end of one famous TV commercial, Iacocca looked directly into the camera and said with friendly confidence and pride, "If you can find a better car, buy it."

He could not have expressed more confidence in his cars than that. Indeed, Iacocca's business success in turning Chrysler around—and his advertising impact as the company's spokesperson—became legendary.

Another of my favorite selling heuristics was developed and used by Dan G., one of my colleagues at Merrill Lynch Asset Management. Through his career, Dan consistently maintained one of the best investment account closing ratios in our firm. Dan is an affable and excellent investment marketing person. His signature closing statement to the client was, "If you don't select us today, it won't be because we are not one of *the most stable organizations in the money management industry.*"

The attribute given emphasis could be one of many. It depended on the client and each situation. His unspoken point was that the attribute he mentioned *should be* of major importance to this or any client. The beauty of what he did was to *ask for the order* while he reinforced our firm's best, most-relevant competitive attribute, linking it directly to the customer's business objectives and their specific matter at hand.

He was confident and credible because he'd offered adequate proof for his assertion, and knew he could deliver the resulting benefit to the client. His comment inspired confidence and definitely helped persuade many prospective clients to use our services, even when we were at a disadvantage on other decision criteria. His success proved to me, once again, that honesty about and confidence in the ability of your product to meet an important client need can go a long way toward producing business success.

Ask for the order.

The presenter's final task is asking for the order. You can craft your own way of making this final point, but there are two things you simply must do. You have to thank your prospective client for the opportunity to present, and then you have to ask for the order.

There are many styles and ways to close. Some of them are *sales heuristics*. But what they have in common is that they are delivered in a confident and credible manner. This is where and why selling yourself first comes into play and why *what you say* may not be as important as *how you say it*.

If you have sold yourself and have a confident posture, the words you actually use will almost take care of themselves. Certainly, they'll have greater impact. It is very hard to conceal personal doubts or insincerity, so do your best to eliminate both by resolving them well before the presentation. As they say in golf, "You have to commit to the shot."

Final thought

Every presenter wants a presentation that addresses their client's needs in a precise, not generic, way. They want to create that perfect product-customer fit—the goal of a bespoke tailor. This is not a fuzzy but a sharp, insightfully informed focus on what is meaningful to the client. This requires presenters to do all that it takes to get that first step right. It is a research/discovery mindset that will provide the insightful knowledge that drives everything else and produces a solution that the customer will want to buy.

That commitment and knowledge informs all downstream aspects of a presentation from its customer relevance, to the presenter's confidence, to the ability to make necessary alterations, to closing the sale.

Providing the perfect fit for your customer's unique matter at hand sets you part from the competition and helps you seal the deal.

Being insightfully knowledgeable about your customer's business objectives is not the only thing, but it's the main thing. When you have that knowledge and adapt to client feedback you are able to continuously make the relevant case needed to be successfully persuasive.

Good luck. And, yes, luck does have something to do with it.

ACKNOWLEDGMENTS

First and foremost, I want to thank my bosses, colleagues and the members of my staff and teams at Young & Rubicam and Merrill Lynch who gave me the support, guidance, and autonomy to help me achieve so many successes in my sales and marketing careers at those firms.

I am also grateful to the many people who contributed their expertise and suggestions in helping me develop the ideas in the book and some of the stories that illustrated them. The book is better because of Alan Andreasen, Ken Bean, Len Berry, Steve Bland, Marly Cornell, Lily Coyle, Arielle Eckstut, Bob Ehret, Mark Higgins, Jim Kennedy, Michael Mitchell, Heather Riemer, John Ryan, Herb Schaffner, John Schaidler, Mike Sobczyk, Andrew Upah, Sydney Upah, Paul Welge, and Golden Zenon. Thank you all.

ABOUT THE AUTHOR

Greg Upah, PhD draws from a wealth of sales and presentation experiences in academia, advertising, and financial services. He was an associate research director and member of the new business team at Young & Rubicam Advertising, New York for seven years. During his career as the director of Institutional Marketing for the asset management group at Merrill Lynch, he successfully established relationships with major corporations and high-net-worth individuals around the globe.

Prior to his careers in advertising and investment management, he was a marketing professor at Virginia Tech and an adjunct associate professor at the Stern School of Business at NYU. He graduated from the University of Notre Dame, and has a PhD in marketing from the University of Illinois at Urbana-Champaign. He has published articles in a variety of journals including the *Journal of Marketing*. He is currently actively involved in helping organizations improve their client presentation capabilities. He lives in Montgomery, Texas.

NOTES

1. Chris Anderson, "How to Give a Killer Presentation: Lessons From TED," *Harvard Business Review*, June 2013.
2. Peter Thiel, *Zero to One: Notes on Startups or How to Build on the Future* (New York: Crown Business, 2014), 130.
3. Lou Shipley, Kirk Arnold, and Dennis Hoffman, 15.387, *Entrepreneurial Sales*, Spring 2015, Massachusetts Institute of Technology, MIT OpenCourseWare, https://ocw.mit.edu. License: Creative Commons. BY-NC-SA.
4. David J. Deming, "The Growing Importance of Social Skills in the Labor Market," NBER Working Paper, No. 21473, August, 2015. 12.
5. David Leonard and Jeff Durr, "B2B Sales Growth: Anemic," *Gallup Business Journal*, September 23, 2016, www.gallup.com/home.aspx.
6. Salesforce Pardot blog comments, "New Research Reveals How to Turn More Prospects into Customers," July 16, 2015, http://www.pardot.com/blog/new-research-reveals-how-to-turn-more-prospects-into-customers/.
7. Jeff Durr and David Leonard, "B2B: Secrets to Big Customer Relationships," *Gallup Business Journal*, May 23, 2017, www.gallup.com/home.aspx.
8. Capital Group Private Client Services, https://www.thecapitalgroup.com/pcs/enjoying-your-wealth.html.
9. Robert Cialdini, *Persuasion: The Psychology of Influence* (New York: William Morrow 2006).
10. Roseanne Bachman, "Persuasion: Why we do it. What it takes to do it well. And why we should care," *Creighton University Magazine* (Fall 2014): 14.
11. Ibid.
12. Charles Duhigg, "What Google Learned From Its Quest to Build the Perfect Team," *The New York Times Magazine*, February 25, 2016.
13. Scott Hartley, *The Fuzzy and the Techie: Why the Liberal Arts Will Rule the Digital World* (Boston: Houghton-Mifflin Harcourt, 2017).
14. Jonathan Horowitz, "Customer Interviews, Just Do it," August 4, 2015, http://bits.citrusbyte.com/customer-interviews-just-do-it/.
15. As of July 29, 2017, this comment was listed on the BlackRock website: "The Global Allocation Fund Outperformed Global Stocks with Less Volatility over Any Ten-Year Period," https://www.blackrock.com/investing/products/227680/blackrock-global-allocation-institutional-class-fund.
16. John Ryan, president, Wright-Ryan Construction, Portland, Maine.

17. Tricia Wang, "The human insights missing from big data," TED Talk, July 19, 2017, https://www.ted.com/talks/tricia_wang_the_human_insights_missing_from_big_data.

18. Simon Sinek, *Start With Why: How Great Leaders Inspire Everyone to Take Action* (New York: Penguin, 2009).

19. Accessed from the Edward Jones website as of July 2017. See https://www.edwardjones.com/value/index.html.

20. Robert Herjavec, *You Don't Have to Be a Shark* (New York: St. Martin's Press, 2016), 143.

21. Norman Bradburn, Seymour Sudman, and Brian Wansink, *Asking Questions*, (San Francisco: Jossey-Bass, 2007), 154–156.

22. Horowitz, Citrusbyte, footnote, 170.

23. Sarah Green Carmichael, "Asking for advice makes people think you're smarter," HBR Ideacast, *Harvard Business Review*, June 2, 2016, https://hbr.org/.

24. Bradburn, Sudman, and Wansink, 2016.

25. Ibid.

26. Horowitz, Citrusbyte, 2015.

27. "Merrill Edge's Online School for Millennials," Barron's Digital Investor Theresa W. Carey, May 29, 2017, http://www.barrons.com/articles/merrills-online-school-plus-tinder-for-investing-1495858754.

28. As indicated on their website as of July 29, 2017, Merrill Lynch suggests that millennials value personal financial advice but are not going to accept advisor claims at face value. See https://pbigaem.fs.ml.com/content/dam/pbig/pdfs/PBIG_millenials-and-money-pdf.

29. Accessed from a Wells Fargo website on July 29, 2017 under the heading: "Wells-Fargo/Gallup Survey: Majority of Investors Continue to Believe American Dream is Achievable." See https://newsroom.wf.com/press-release/wealth-and-investment-management/wells-fargogallup-survey-majority-investors-continue.

30. On May 23, 2016, ESPN posted these comments on their website under the title: "You Won't Believe How Nike Lost Steph to Under Armour."

31. Cialdini, *Persuasion*.

32. Lou Shipley, Kirk Arnold, and Dennis Hoffman, 2015.

33. Accessed from the Gieves and Hawkes website, June 1, 2017. See http://www.gievesandhawkes.com/.

34. David Leonard and Jeff Durr, 2016.

35. Daniel Kahneman, *Thinking, Fast and Slow* (New York: Farrar, Straus and Giroux, 2011), 64.

36. Chris Anderson, "How to Give a Killer Presentation: Lessons From TED," *Harvard Business Review*, June 2013.

37. Anderson, *Harvard Business Review*, 2013.

38. See https://www.raymondjames.com/about-us.

39. Nancy Duarte, *Slide-Ology: The Art and Science of Creating Great Presentations* (Boston: Harvard Business School Publishing), 2.

40. Ian Parker, "Absolute PowerPoint," *The New Yorker*, May 28, 2001.

41. Ibid.

42. *Microsoft by the Numbers. See* https://news.microsoft.com/bythenumbers/.

43. Carmine Gallo. *Talk Like TED: The 9 Presentation Secrets of the World's Top Minds*, (New York: St. Martin's Griffin, 2015), 191.

44. Lou Shipley, Kirk Arnold, and Dennis Hoffman, 2015.

45. Bachman, 2014.

46. Aaron Caroll, "To Be Sued Less, Doctors Should Consider Talking to Patients More," *The New York Times*, June 1, 2015.

47. Hartley, 2016.

48. Sinek, *Start With Why*, 17.

49. Adrienne Carter, Amy Feldman, and Jason Zweig, "Putnam: The Greed Machine," *Money Magazine,* November 21, 2003.

50. Ibid.

51. David Leonard and Jeff Durr, 2016.

52. Arlene Jacobius, "DC Participants Reacting to Market," *Pensions and Investments*, May 15, 2000.